the Botany of Desire

OUR SURPRISING RELATIONSHIP WITH PLANTS

MICHAEL POLLAN
with RICHIE CHEVAT

Rocky Pond Books

ROCKY POND BOOKS
An imprint of Penguin Random House LLC, New York

First published in the United States of America by Rocky Pond Books,
an imprint of Penguin Random House LLC, 2023
First paperback edition published 2024

Rocky Pond Books & colophon are trademarks of Penguin Random House LLC.
The Penguin colophon is a registered trademark of Penguin Books Limited.

Visit us online at PenguinRandomHouse.com.

THE LIBRARY OF CONGRESS HAS CATALOGED THE HARDCOVER EDITION AS FOLLOWS:
Names: Pollan, Michael, author. | Hornik, Lauri, editor.
Title: The botany of desires : our surprising relationship with plants /
Michael Pollan ; with Lauri Hornik.
Other titles: Botany of desires (Young reader's adaptation)
Description: New York City : Rocky Pond Books, 2023. |
Includes bibliographical references and index. | Audience: Ages 10–14 |
Audience: Grades 7–9 | Summary: "In this entertaining young readers edition of
the environmental studies classic, Michael Pollan demonstrates how people and
domesticated plants have formed a reciprocal relationship"—Provided by publisher.
Identifiers: LCCN 2023037274 (print) | LCCN 2023037275 (ebook) |
ISBN 9780593531525 (hardcover) | ISBN 9780593531549 (trade paperback) |
ISBN 9780593531532 (ebook)
Subjects: LCSH: Human-plant relationships—Juvenile literature.
Classification: LCC QK46.5.H85 P66 2023 (print) | LCC QK46.5.H85 (ebook)
| DDC 581.6/3—dc23/eng/20231005
LC record available at https://lccn.loc.gov/2023037274
LC ebook record available at https://lccn.loc.gov/2023037275

Printed in the United States of America
ISBN 9780593531549
1st Printing

LSCC

Design by Sylvia Bi | Text set in Apollo MT Pro

Contents

Preface

Every now and then an idea comes along that changes everything—or at least, everything about how you look at the world. For me, it is the idea at the heart of this book, an idea that is about to infect you.

One of the weirdest things about being human is our so-called relationship to nature. The weirdness is embedded in that very phrase: To have "a relationship to nature" implies that we somehow stand outside it, and from that mythical position "relate" to it. Yet we humans are animals who evolved just like every other species. We are fully a part of nature, even if we seldom feel that way.

Maybe it's our arrogance, the belief that we are somehow special and therefore above it all. We feel powerful in nature, for better and worse. We manipulate other species in all sorts of ways, and have altered the landscape and earth's ecosystem so dramatically that we have caused a new geologic era called The Anthropocene.

I suppose it's nice to feel special and powerful, but it leads to all sorts of problems—including the environmental crisis we now find ourselves in. I don't believe we can begin to resolve this crisis until we completely rethink our place in nature. That means learning to see ourselves as one creature among many, and regarding other creatures not as unfeeling objects for us to exploit, but as fellow beings with their own interests, intelligence, and perspectives that are deserving of our respect.

This is the idea at the heart of this book, which I think of as offering a plant's-eye view of the world. One of our greatest blessings as humans is our imagination, which allows us to put ourselves in the shoes (or roots) of other creatures, the better to see the world from their perspectives. That's what you will learn to do as you read this book—see how, far from being the passive objects of our attentions, plants are busy with their own agendas. And for many of them, especially the ones we arrogantly call "domesticated," that means getting animals like us to do things for them they can't do for themselves: spread their genes around the world, clear land and create new habitat for them, and then care for them. The question of who's really in charge here is a live one, and the answer will surprise you.

When we begin to see the world, and ourselves, from the plant's point of view, everything changes. We gain new respect for the ingenuity of plants, and begin to develop a more realistic (and humbler) sense of our own role and powers in nature. You will come to see that these other creatures have evolved the ability to use us even as we use them—and that the same goes for domestic animals and even the trillions of bacteria with whom you share your body. All of us participate in this great, big, beautiful dance of symbiosis, partners in co-evolution, changing and being changed, mutually dependent. The sooner we recognize that we're all in this together, the sooner we can begin to repair the damage our mistaken ideas of specialness and power have created. There's no time to lose.

Introduction: The Bees and Me

The seeds of this book were first planted in my garden—while I was planting seeds, as a matter of fact. Sowing seed can be relaxing. It's not hard, and it leaves you plenty of mental space to think about other things while you're doing it.

On that spring afternoon, I happened to be sowing potatoes next to a flowering apple tree that was vibrating with bees. They buzzed from flower to flower and together they made a noise like a small engine. Listening to them, I was struck by this idea: Weren't we (the bees and I) doing basically the same thing? Both of us were helping plants to reproduce.

The bees, while going after the sweet nectar in the flower, were spreading pollen from one bloom to another. The pollinated flowers would then grow into fruit (apples) with a star-shaped pattern of seeds inside. Those seeds, under the right conditions, could become new apple trees. Though I had nothing to do with creating my potato seeds, by planting and tending to them, I was also helping new plants to grow.

Of course, the bee doesn't know that it's helping to create new apple trees. I, on the other hand, am very aware of what I'm doing. I carefully plan my garden, deciding which seeds to plant, where and how many. In my garden, I'm in charge. If one year I decide to plant leeks and not potatoes, then that's what gets planted. I'm helped by a long chain of other people who are making decisions: botanists who develop the seeds I plant, gardeners whose knowledge guides me in my decisions, agricultural scientists who breed new types of potatoes.

But what struck me that day, as I listened to the buzzing of the bees, was that maybe, despite all the decisions and choices we humans make, our situation really isn't different from that of the bees. The apple tree has lured the bee into working for it spreading its genes—by the promise of nectar. The bee has no idea it has been manipulated by the tree. So I wondered: Have I been manipulated by the potato too?

Did I choose to plant these potatoes, or did the potato make me do it?

We tend to think of the bee as an unwitting servant of the flower, almost as if it is "tricked" into helping the plant reproduce. But in fact, the bee and the flower are partners. Each gets something out of the arrangement. The bee gets food in the form of nectar and the flower gets help in reproducing. They each need the other. Without bees (or other pollinators), there will be no new seeds and no new flowers. Without flowers and the food they provide, no new bees.

This relationship is an example of what scientists call "coevolution." Flowering plants and pollinators like bees and wasps evolved together over millions of years. Neither of them planned for it to happen, but over time they became dependent on each other.

Our relationship to the potato (or any of the other plants we use) isn't much different. We both get something from the arrangement. We get food from the potato and—here is the point we often overlook—the potato gets help in reproducing.

Let's spend a moment thinking about that.

We like to think we're in charge, it's all about us, we use the potato, we grow the potato, we change and breed the potato to suit our needs. Yet it is undeniable, that just like the bee and the flower, our relationship with the potato is a two-way street. Potatoes offer humans an easily grown source of food. In return, we humans have helped the potato spread from a limited area high in the Andes of South America until now, when it is grown (and eaten) all over the world. Humans and the potato are partners. Both benefit from the relationship. (I'm talking about the potato as a species or type of plant. Obviously, it doesn't help individual potatoes to be baked, roasted, or chopped up and fried in oil.)

Looking at it this way takes human beings out of the center of the story. We are no longer the bosses, the decision makers, the ones in charge. Instead, we are part of a complex web of relationships with the natural world. Did I choose to plant potatoes, or did potatoes get me to plant them? Am I using the potato, or is it using me?

Both are true. That idea—that humans and plants exist in partnership—is the central theme of this book.

Plant Partners

This book looks at four plants that have greatly benefited from their partnership with humans—the apple, the tulip, coffee, and the potato. They are all what we call "domesticated species," but, as we will see, that can be a misleading term. Yes, we have learned to use these plants, and we've changed them to make them better suit our needs. But looking at it from the plants' point of view, it's just as true to say they have used us.

The wild ancestors of these plants—the wild tulip, the wild potato—didn't look much like their domesticated offspring. But each had the potential to satisfy some human need or desire. They were also relatively easy for humans to grow and adapt. The apple was good at providing humans with a taste of sweetness before sugar was widely available. The tulip satisfies our desire for beauty. Coffee gives us a boost of energy and a sense of well-being. The potato has become a basic food source around the world.

Evolution is sometimes described as "survival of the fittest." That can give the mistaken impression that it's all about competition. Plants and animals compete for food or sunlight and the best one wins. But evolution isn't merely driven by competition. There are many, many examples in nature of cooperation between species, of animals that have evolved together to the point where they need each other for survival.

Clown fish (like Nemo in *Finding Nemo*) clean sea anemones, and in turn the stinging anemones provide protection from predators. Cows rely on bacteria in their gut to digest cellulose in grasses. In return the bacteria have a safe environment and a reliable food supply. There are hundreds if not thousands of other examples, including our own partnerships with plants and animals. There's nothing more natural. It's just as natural as the cooperation between the bee and the flower.

We are so used to the domesticated plants and animals we live among, we have stopped thinking of them as part of the natural world. We may even look down on them a little. Maybe it's that word *domesticated*. We love our dogs, but we respect the wolf more. We think the dog is our tamed servant, but the wolf is wild and free.

But what is a dog? It's a wolf that has evolved to be able to live with humans. You may not recognize it when you look at a toy poodle or a bulldog, but that's what it is. Dogs are the descendants of wolves that were less aggressive and were willing to let people approach them. Those friendlier wolves benefited by getting the scraps of food humans gave them. Humans benefited by having watchdogs, hunting dogs, and companions. Over time, those friendlier wolves evolved into dogs. That evolutionary strategy has been amazingly successful. There are fifty million dogs in America today, but only ten thousand wolves.

In the same way, the domesticated plants like rice, corn, wheat, potatoes, and soybeans are the amazing success stories of the botanical world. Looking at it from the plants' point of view, humans have done a great job at helping them reproduce and spread. Along the way, they have (with human help) adapted and changed to meet human needs even better. For example, the potato was transformed from a tiny, toxic root into a fat, nourishing food, and the tulip started as a short, unremarkable wildflower and became a tall, eye-catching beauty.

And while we have changed them, these plants have changed us as well. Each of the plants in this book has an incredible story that is part of human history. The introduction of coffee to Europe changed society and may have helped spark the Industrial Revolution. The potato became the staple food for poor people in Europe until it was struck by a disease, leading to terrible famine and emigration. In seventeenth-century Holland, in an early example of market mania, tulip bulbs briefly became worth more than their weight in gold.

The shape and size of the modern potato or the colors of a modern tulip can tell us a lot about the intertwined history of humans and plants. What did tulip breeders in Holland think was beautiful three hundred years ago? Why do we want golden potatoes rather than purple ones? What did the apple mean to Americans who were pushing into Native American land in the 1800s? These are all part of the story of plants and people.

The Genius of Plants

The partnership between plants and humans is only possible because a hundred million years ago, plants evolved a new way of reproducing—by getting animals to help them. This was an amazing step because plants can't move about; they are, by nature, rooted in one spot. Earlier plants used the wind to carry their seeds to new areas. But then, through the random trial and error of evolution, plants stumbled on a way—actually a few thousand different ways—of getting animals to carry their genes.

This new class of plants made showy flowers and formed large seeds that attracted animals. They evolved burrs that attach to animal fur like Velcro, flowers that offered nectar to insects, and acorns that squirrels collect and bury and, just often enough, forget to eat.

Then, about ten thousand years ago, an animal was not only attracted to the seeds and fruits of flowering plants but began to think about and plan how to grow more of the ones it liked. That animal was, of course, us. This is often referred to as the "invention of agriculture," but you might just as well call it "the invention of plants harnessing humans."

Consider this: For millions of years grasses and trees have been locked in an ongoing battle for space and sunlight. The grasses relied on herbivores, plant-eating animals, to keep the forest from invading their turf. But they couldn't invade the forest—there wasn't enough light for them to grow. Then something happened that tipped the balance of power toward the grasslands. Humans found edible grasses such as wheat and corn and rice useful and tasty, so we cut down vast forests to make more room for them. The triumph of the grasses is still going on as forests are cut down to make new habitats for them, with devastating consequences for climate change.

How are plants able to attract animals and get them to spread their seeds? By being masters of chemistry—far better at it than we are. Plants live by transforming sunlight, water, and soil into an astonishing variety of substances. They make their own food and their own cells. They produce insecticides to repel harmful creatures and fragrances to attract helpful ones. They make chemical signals to communicate with other plants and insects. And they cooperate with many other organisms, especially fungi, in the soil.

These same tactics worked on us humans. We were attracted by their fruits and seeds, their colors and fragrances. And over generations we learned that many of the plants' chemical inventions are helpful to us. Compounds invented by plants can heal us, help us stay awake, or satisfy our sweet tooth.

Plants didn't *plan* to make chemicals that humans found useful. It happened by accident, as a by-product of their need for chemical defenses or to attract pollinators. But that's the way nature and evolution work. It turned out, purely by chance, that humans and certain kinds of plants were very helpful to each other. When we worked as partners with those plants, both of us benefited.

This book tells the story of four of those partnerships. But it also tells a bigger story; the story of the interconnected relationship between human beings and nature. Often, we see ourselves in opposition to the natural world. It's the view that puts us at the center—the bosses, the deciders—while the natural world is something that must be tamed or domesticated or simply used. In this way of looking at the world, humanity stands apart, separate from nature.

This book tells a different kind of story, one that aims to put us back in the great interconnected web that is life on Earth. My hope is that by the time you close this book's cover, things will look a little different to you. I hope that when you see an apple tree across a road or a tulip across a table, you'll recognize these plants as active partners in a great collaboration. Maybe you won't go so far as to think of yourself as a bee, but you'll understand that, like the bee, we are tied to plants and the natural world by a million invisible bonds.

Chapter One

Desire: *Sweetness*
Plant: *The Apple*

Imagine yourself on the banks of the Ohio River in the spring of 1806, somewhere just north of Wheeling, West Virginia. The river is wide and brown, and its steep shores are thick with oaks and hickories. But it's not empty. A constant fleet of canoes, barges, and other river craft go by. The boats are carrying a steady stream of American colonizers who are pushing into Native American lands west of Pennsylvania.

As you stand there, you see a strange makeshift boat drifting by. It stands out for two reasons. First, you notice the way it is made—out of two hollowed-out logs lashed together, a double canoe. Second, you see the skinny white man of about thirty, dozing in one of the canoes without a care in the world. He's just snoozing, letting the river take him where it wants to go.

The other hull is riding low in the water, weighed down by a small mountain of seeds. The seeds have been carefully blanketed with moss and mud to keep them from drying out in the sun. Now you realize who the sleeping man is. His name is John Chapman, but everyone knows him by his nickname: Johnny Appleseed.

Even in his own time, Johnny Appleseed was a legend, a folk hero. Among other things, he was known as an animal lover, a vegetarian, a deeply religious person, a loner but one who liked to talk to people, and a successful businessman. People who knew him say he always went barefoot and wore an old coffee sack like a poncho and a tin pot for a hat. But what he's most famous for, of course, is planting thousands of apple trees across what would become Ohio and Indiana.

Chapman would collect bushels of seeds from waste piles at

cider mills in Pennsylvania. One bushel would have been enough to plant more than three hundred thousand trees. Then he would ferry them in his double-hulled canoe, down the Ohio River, planting orchards, sometimes on land he owned and sometimes on land he didn't. When new colonizers arrived, they would find Chapman waiting for them, ready to sell them apple trees that were already two or three years old.

The story of John Chapman, "Johnny Appleseed," has stuck in my mind since I first learned about him years ago. To me it's a story that captures the partnership between people and plants. Chapman seems to have understood this, that he was working for the apples as much as they were working for him. Perhaps that's why he sometimes compared himself to a bumblebee. Maybe that's where I got the idea that I too was like a bee, when I was planting potatoes in my garden.

Chapman's boat was a perfect symbol of his attitude. Instead of towing his shipment of seeds behind him, he lashed the two hulls together so they would travel down the river side by side, equal partners. Thanks to that partnership, the apple got John Chapman to spread it across the Midwest. In return, John Chapman got . . . well, that is an interesting part of the story.

As American as Apple Pie?

Like Johnny Appleseed, the apple itself has become so woven into the story of the United States that it's easy to forget it's not native to North America. It was brought to this hemisphere by European colonists. Yet, like so many immigrants, the apple has firmly rooted itself on this continent. Along the way, its fate has become tied up with that of people.

Other trees, like the oak, have done very well without human help. Acorns, the fruit of oak trees, are highly nutritious, but they're far too bitter for us to eat. Instead, oaks have a fine partnership with squirrels, who bury acorns for winter food and then forget about one-quarter of them. (That number comes from Beatrix Potter, who wrote the Peter Rabbit books, so it may not be completely accurate.) Whatever the real number is, squirrels spread oak seeds in return for the acorns they eat.

The apple, however, has proven much more adaptable to human needs. It comes in so many varieties that people have been able to find many uses for it. Meanwhile, the apple hasn't just become a part of our diet. It has also become a part of our culture. Today, an apple is a symbol of health, wholesomeness, and even patriotism. We say, "An apple a day keeps the doctor away," or that something is "as American as apple pie."

When I started this book, I wanted to understand how the apple had made such a successful partnership with human beings. I wanted to find out how this fruit had earned such a unique place in our lives. And what better place to start than with the story of Johnny Appleseed?

Today, we think of apples as the perfect example of sweetness and goodness. Likewise, John Chapman—Johnny Appleseed— is looked upon as an almost saint-like figure, bringing goodness

17

and "civilization" to the "wilderness." But the truth is something stranger and more interesting.

John Chapman, Oddball

I began my search on a summery October afternoon about two hundred years after John Chapman's first trip. I went to a bank of the Ohio River a few miles south of Steubenville, Ohio. That is the exact spot where Chapman is thought to have first set foot in the state. (At the time, several Midwest states, including Ohio and Indiana, were called the Northwest Territory.) My plan was to track down the sites of Chapman's orchards, follow his footsteps (and canoe wake), and see if maybe I could find one of the trees he planted.

I had read a biography of Chapman by Robert Price, so I already knew that the real Johnny Appleseed was not as simple or as cute as the one in children's storybooks. Price describes him as a man who "had the thick bark of queerness on him." The facts bear that out.

Chapman moved west from Longmeadow, Massachusetts, in 1797, at the age of twenty-three. That seems to have been the last time he had a fixed address or real home. He preferred to spend his nights out of doors. He was a vegetarian at a time when that was very unusual. He was a passionate nature lover. He thought it was cruel to ride a horse or chop down a tree. He once punished his own foot for squashing a worm by throwing away its shoe.

A lot of Chapman's behavior can be explained by the fact that he was a deeply religious man following the teachings of Emanuel Swedenborg. Swedenborg was a Protestant philosopher in the 1700s who taught that everything on Earth corresponds directly to something in the afterlife. That means that everything is sacred, whether it's a tree or a worm.

Chapman's kindness to animals was legendary. It was said he would put out his campfire if he thought insects were being attracted to it. He often bought lame horses to save them from slaughter. Once he freed a wolf he found snared in a trap, nursing it to health and then keeping it as a pet.

It seems he could sleep anywhere, though he preferred hollowed-out logs or a hammock slung between two trees. One evening he was planning to sleep in a log, but when he discovered there were bear cubs living in it, he slept in the snow instead. One whole winter he set up house in a hollowed-out sycamore stump. Then there was the time he floated a hundred miles down the Allegheny River on a block of ice, sleeping the whole way.

A great many stories about him have to do with his feet. They say he'd go barefoot in any weather. He would entertain children by pressing needles or hot coals into the soles of his feet, which had grown as horny and tough as an elephant's. These stories show that people understood that Chapman's relationship to nature was special. He wanted nothing between him and the earth, not even the protective barrier of shoes. Like the animals he loved, he wanted his feet rooted in the dirt.

His fellow colonists regarded him as an oddball, to say the

least. He was a loner who never married. To people who asked why, he would say that God had promised him a "true wife in Heaven." Yet despite his peculiar attire and personal habits, he was a popular figure. People were happy to have him as a guest in their homes, and parents would let him bounce their babies on his lap.

Pioneers or Colonizers?

History often depicts Chapman and his fellow colonizers as "pioneers" taming an uncharted "wilderness," but that is far from the truth. Chapman and the other colonizers were living on land that belonged to tribes including Haudenosaunee (Iroquois), Lenape (Delaware), Wyandot, Shawnee, and Miami people. The countryside was dotted with Native American villages and towns, connected by well-worn trails and pathways. The landscape wasn't wild; it had been carefully tended and cultivated by the people living there for many generations.

Native Americans had time and again resisted the spread of white colonists into their land. They had fought a series of wars with the British and later with the new United States. The largest of these wars was Pontiac's Rebellion in 1763, when a broad alliance of tribes fought the British. The war lasted for two years and stopped the western expansion of the colonists for a time. But by 1806, when John Chapman arrived, the tide of colonization had long since resumed.

I brought a copy of Robert Price's biography of John Chapman with me to Ohio. I used the maps in the book to retrace Chapman's annual migration from western Pennsylvania to his properties in Ohio and, later, Indiana. It was Price's book that led me to the spot where Chapman first landed in Ohio, in a tiny town now called Brilliant.

The book mentions a stream called George's Run that emptied into the Ohio. But when I arrived in Brilliant no one had heard of it. Eventually I discovered that the stream had long since been rerouted through a large concrete pipe. Today George's Run flows underground, passes a used-car dealership, crosses beneath a potholed street, and finally reemerges from the earth halfway down a steep, littered embankment behind a convenience store. From there it contributes its meager trickle to the Ohio River.

We can be sure that John Chapman found a very different scene when he showed up with his double-sided canoe and mounds of seeds. There was already a small settlement of white colonists and they urged him to stay and plant a nursery. But Chapman had other plans. He preferred to stay just ahead of the settlers. He'd find a place where the colonists hadn't arrived, plant a nursery, and wait. By the time the tide of new arrivals found him, he'd have young apple trees ready to sell them. Then he'd hire a local boy to look after his nursery and move farther on to start all over again.

Thanks to this strategy, by the 1830s Chapman was operating a chain of nurseries that reached all the way from western Pennsylvania through central Ohio and into Indiana. When he died in Fort Wayne in 1845, he owned some 1,200 acres of prime real estate. The barefoot oddball died a wealthy man.

Appleseed's Appleseeds

When I considered the story of John "Appleseed" Chapman, one thing stood out. As his name tells us, he wasn't carrying little apple trees in his canoe, he was carrying apple *seeds*. And, as any apple farmer will tell you, if you plant an apple seed, you have no way of telling what the apples on the new tree will taste like.

Slice an apple through at its middle and you will find five small chambers arrayed in a perfect starburst. Each of the chambers holds a seed, sometimes two. They are such a deep, shiny brown, they look as if they've been oiled and polished by a woodworker. Two facts about these seeds are worth noting:

First, apple seeds contain a small quantity of the poison cyanide. This makes them almost indescribably bitter. This is probably a defense the apple evolved to discourage animals from biting into them. The trees want you to eat their fruit but not chew on the seeds, so they can survive to grow into new trees.

The second, more important fact about apple seeds is their genetic content. Every seed in an apple contains the genetic instructions for a completely new and different apple tree. Plant an apple seed and the tree that grows bears only the slightest resemblance to its parent. This was true of every seed riding down the Ohio alongside John Chapman. Apples grown from those seeds would likely be so sour, they would be almost inedible. As the writer and naturalist Henry David Thoreau once said, they would be "sour enough to set a squirrel's teeth on edge and make a jay scream."

The botanical term for this is "heterozygosity," which roughly means variable offspring. We humans are like this. Children are not identical to their parents. But in the apple the tendency is extreme. Each seed, even from the same apple, can grow into a very different kind of apple tree.

Wherever the apple tree goes, its offspring come in an amazing array of variations, at least five per apple, several thousand per tree. All that variety makes it likely that at least a couple of young trees will have whatever qualities it takes to prosper in the surrounding climate and soil. More than any other single trait, it is the apple's genetic variability that accounts for its capacity to make itself at home in places as different as New England and New Zealand, central Asia and California.

But this means the way to reproduce your favorite apple tree isn't by seed. It's by an ancient technique called grafting. Grafting involves taking a branch from one tree and getting it to grow on a root or branch taken from a second tree. In other words, you take a part of the original and make it grow into a new but identical tree. The flowers and fruit of the grafted branch stay the same.

If not for grafting, every apple in the world would be its own distinct variety. All commercial apples that you buy in a store are grown from grafted trees. Name your favorite apple, whether it's Fuji, Honeycrisp, Granny Smith, or some other variety. Without grafting, that apple would disappear when the tree it grew on died.

But if John Chapman's seeds were unpredictable, and everyone knew it, why did he find eager customers for his trees among the newly arriving settlers? The answer may be surprising if not a little shocking. The colonists didn't mean to eat the apples; they meant to turn them into hard cider. Apples were something people drank, not as juice but as alcohol.

Drinking Apples

Here's a fact you won't hear in most stories about Johnny Appleseed. Early Americans drank an enormous amount of alcohol. Most adults and even sometimes children consumed some at every meal. One reason was that water supplies weren't always pure. Alcohol killed the microbes in water, making it safer to drink.

Cider, an alcoholic drink made from apples, was extremely popular. (Today we call cider that contains alcohol hard cider, but in the early years of the country, all cider was alcoholic.) Apples were easier to grow than grapes, and their flesh was full of sugars that could be fermented to produce alcohol.

Colonists also made alcohol from corn, called corn liquor, or "white lightning." However, after the apple trees began to bear fruit, cider—being safer, tastier, and much easier to make—became the alcoholic drink of choice. Just about the only reason to plant an orchard from the sort of seeds John Chapman was selling would have been to turn the fruits into intoxicating drinks.

Allowed to ferment for a few weeks, pressed apple juice yields a mildly alcoholic beverage with about half the strength of wine. For something stronger, the cider can then be distilled into apple brandy. (Distilling involves boiling off some of the water so the alcohol content is higher.) Or the cider can simply be left outside to freeze out the water. The liquor that is left is called applejack.

Virtually every homestead in America had an orchard from which gallons of cider were made every year. In rural areas cider took the place not only of wine and beer but of coffee and tea, juice, and even water.

That is, until the late 1800s. There had always been people who believed that consuming alcohol was wrong or even sinful, but after the Civil War, a social movement began to grow based on that idea. It was called the temperance movement, or the women's temperance movement because its most vocal leaders were women. This movement for prohibition—that is, the banning of alcohol—also overlapped somewhat with the movement for women's rights, the women's suffrage movement.

However, cider was so indispensable to rural life that at first those who preached against the evil of alcohol made an exception for cider. The early prohibitionists succeeded mainly in switching drinkers over from whiskey or other grain liquor to apple spirits.

By the late 1800s a woman named Carry Nation was a leader

of the temperance movement. She was famous for marching into bars with her followers and smashing bottles and furniture with a hatchet. As the temperance movement grew in strength, it began to target cider and they began to chop down apple trees as well. Some of those trees had probably been planted by John Chapman.

In the face of the growing temperance movement, apple growers knew they needed to rebrand the fruit. Instead of a source of alcohol, they wanted it thought of as something innocent and nutritious. They launched a public relations campaign promoting a new, more family-friendly view of the apple. With slogans like "An apple a day keeps the doctor away," they successfully transformed it into a symbol of health and wholesomeness.

Of course, the true story of Johnny Appleseed had to be transformed also. In place of an oddball who planted apple trees for cider, he became a sort of backwoods saint, bringing wholesomeness and civilization to the wilderness.

The temperance movement would achieve a great, if short-lived, victory. Starting in 1920, alcohol was outlawed in the United States. That failed experiment was called Prohibition and only lasted until 1933. But it forever changed the way we think of the apple and of Johnny Appleseed.

From Asia to America

The ancestor of *Malus domestica*—the domesticated apple— is a wild apple that grows in the mountains of Kazakhstan in central Asia. In some places there you will find entire forests of wild apple trees. The trees grow up to sixty feet tall and carry fruits ranging in size from marbles to softballs. These wild apples sprout in a riot of colors: yellow, green, red, and purple. If you saw them, you might not recognize them as apples at all.

The old Silk Road, an ancient trading route that stretched from China to the Mediterranean, went through some of these wild apple forests. It seems likely that travelers passing through would have picked the biggest and tastiest of the fruits to take with them. Along the way seeds were dropped, and trees grew up. Those trees mixed freely with other apple varieties, such as the European crab apples. Eventually there were millions of apple trees all through Asia and Europe. Most of them would have produced bitter, inedible fruit. Though as we've seen, even those apples could be used for cider, or as animal feed.

On its own, that was the best the apple could do—get humans to spread its seeds. Then sometime before the year 1,000 BCE people in China invented grafting. They discovered that a small branch of wood cut from a desirable tree could be notched into the trunk of another tree. This grafted branch would join with the new trunk.

A grafted tree isn't really the child of the original, but more like a clone. Its new branches, flowers, and fruit are exactly the same as the tree from which it was taken. Genetically, at least, you can say it's the same tree.

Grafting allowed people to save and reproduce apple varieties they liked. (Or any other fruit, for that matter.) As we've seen, growing apple trees from seed is a complete gamble. You never know what the new apples will taste like. The new technique of grafting guaranteed growers could keep getting the same apples, even if the old tree died.

The ancient Greeks and Romans knew about grafting (maybe the knowledge was carried along the Silk Road). They used it to select and grow the choicest specimens of apples. The Romans cultivated at least twenty-three different varieties, some of which they took with them when they conquered Britain. The tiny, squat Lady apple, which still shows up in US markets in December, is thought to be one of these.

From the ancient world to Europe, the apple then crossed the Atlantic, carried by European colonizers. The earliest immigrants to North America brought grafted European apple trees with them, but most of those fared poorly in their new home. Harsh winters killed off many of them. The fruit of others was nipped in the bud by late-spring frosts unknown in Europe.

However, the colonists also planted seeds, often saved from apples eaten during their Atlantic passage. Those seedling trees, called "pippins," eventually prospered, especially after the colonists imported honeybees to improve pollination. Thanks to the apple's great genetic diversity, some of the seeds from the new trees were better suited to life in their new home than others. They were also probably helped by genetic mixing with the native American crab apple.

This gave the European colonists new, American apple varieties they could then spread through grafting. Besides the Newtown

Pippin, there were Baldwins, Golden Russets, and Jonathans. In a remarkably short period of time, the New World had its own apples, adapted to the soil and climate and length of day of North America. Ben Franklin reported that by 1781 the fame of the Newtown Pippin, a homegrown apple discovered in a Flushing, New York, cider orchard, had already spread to Europe.

From Seed to Settlement

The apple followed the advance of European colonists as they pushed farther west into Native American lands. It was the same trail John Chapman followed in the early years of the United States, from New England to western Pennsylvania to the Ohio River valley. Like Chapman, I too followed the course of the Ohio River as it wound south toward the town of Marietta, Ohio.

As the river flows along, the landscape begins to relax. The steep, rocky hillsides that leap up from the river near Wheeling, West Virginia, merge into rolling, rich-looking farmland. In some fields you can see an old-time oil derrick. The first oil fields in America were found just outside Marietta. Farmers digging a well noticed bubbles of natural gas coming up through the water.

Marietta was founded in 1788 by a Revolutionary War hero named Rufus Putnam and a small party of men. Their families would follow a few months later, after the men had constructed a small walled settlement. By 1801, Marietta was the gateway for white settlers entering the Northwest Territory. It was also the site of an apple orchard.

Soon after his arrival, Rufus Putnam had planted a nursery on the opposite bank of the Ohio. From that orchard, he sold trees to the pioneers passing through. This means that John Chapman didn't introduce apples to the Northwest Territory. They were already there when he arrived. What's more, the trees Putnam sold were not grown from seeds: They were grafted trees. His nursery offered a selection of the well-known eastern varieties like the Roxbury Russets, Newtown Pippins, and Early Chandlers. Colonizers arriving from back east would have recognized the names and the apples.

Strangely, Chapman would have nothing to do with grafted trees. Apparently, he believed it was wicked to cut trees for grafting and that only God could improve the apple. It's also likely that he stuck to seeds because he liked their portability. As we've seen, once he had an orchard established, he just took his seeds on to the next place, staying one step ahead of the westward push of the settlers. You couldn't pack up an orchard and move when a neighborhood got too crowded.

If you had the temperament for it and didn't care about starting a family or putting down roots, selling apple trees along the shifting edge of white settlement was not a bad business. Apples were precious on the frontier, and Chapman could be sure of a strong demand for his seedlings, even if most of them would yield nothing but spitters. He was selling, cheaply, something everybody wanted—something, in fact, everybody in Ohio needed by law.

The arriving homesteaders weren't just randomly picking out parcels of land to settle on. The US government was giving out land grants, assigning settlers to specific parcels in the Northwest Territory. But to get ownership of the land, the colonists had to fulfill the government requirements. One of these was to "set out at least fifty apple or pear trees." The purpose of the rule was to make sure the homesteaders didn't just sell the land that had been given them for free. The government wanted the new arrivals to put down roots—literally.

A standard apple tree planted from seed normally took ten years to fruit. Planting an orchard was a sign you were planning to stick around, and it became one of the earliest ceremonies of white settlement. The ordered rows of trees were a statement that the colonists were putting their mark on the landscape. The apples also reminded them of their homes back in the eastern states. It must have been comforting to them to think that someday this new territory would resemble the towns they had left behind.

The Treasure of Sweetness

It takes a leap of the imagination to appreciate just how much the apple meant to those people living two hundred years ago. By comparison, the apple in our eye is fairly unimportant. Yes, it's a popular fruit (second only to the banana), but it's nothing we can't live without. But imagine living without the experience of sweetness. Think of how much we enjoy and desire the taste of sweetness on our tongues. That sensation, the chance to taste something sweet, is what the apple represented to Americans in the early 1800s.

Sugar was a rarity in early America. Even after cane plantations were established in the Caribbean, sugar remained a luxury good beyond the reach of most Americans. Also, sugarcane was grown by enslaved Africans. As more and more people, especially in the north, grew opposed to slavery, many avoided buying sugar on principle.

Before the English arrived, there were no honeybees in North America, therefore no honey. Native Americans boiled maple sap to make maple sugar. European settlers carried on that practice. But it wasn't until late in the nineteenth century that sugar became plentiful and cheap enough to be within reach of average Americans. Before then, the sensation of sweetness in the lives of most people came chiefly from eating fruit. And in America that usually meant the apple.

Sweetness in those days was so rare and so special that it came to symbolize a kind of perfection. The word *sweet* meant much more than the taste of sweetness on your tongue. Anything that was good or gave pleasure was said to be sweet. The best land was said to be sweet; so were the most pleasing sounds, the loveliest views, and the most refined people. When Shakespeare called spring the "sweet o' the year," he meant it was the best part of the year. We still sometimes use the word that way. If your friend tells you they got a new bike, you might respond with the exclamation "Sweet!"

To recapture the power of sweetness and the power of the apple, we have to imagine a world where the taste of sugar is rare and astonishing. The closest I've ever come to experiencing that was watching my son at his first birthday party. The icing on the birthday cake was his very first taste of sugar. His face was immediately transformed into an expression of pure surprise and delight. He was on my lap, and I was delivering the forkfuls of sweetness to his gaping mouth. Between bites he gazed up at me in amazement. It was as if he was saying, "The world contains *this*? From this day forward I shall dedicate my life to it."

Cultures around the world vary enormously in their liking for bitter, sour, and salty flavors, but a taste for sweetness appears to be universal. This goes for many animals too, which shouldn't be surprising, since sugar is the form in which nature stores food energy. That is why sweetness is such a force in evolution. Many animals, including us, just can't get enough of it. By encasing their seeds in sugary and nutritious fruits, plants like the apple hit on a way of harnessing the animal sweet tooth. In exchange for sugar, animals provide the seeds with transportation, allowing the plant to expand its range.

There's a lot that goes into making this partnership work. For example, it does the apple no good if animals eat the fruit before the seeds are ready. That's why an unripe apple isn't sweet, and it isn't red. It changes, or *ripens*, when the seeds inside are mature and ready to grow into new trees. Also, as we've seen, the seeds contain a tiny amount of poison and are bitter. That ensures that animals won't chew them but swallow them whole. And the seeds are protected by a hard shell, so they can survive traveling through an animal's digestive tract until they are "deposited" out the other end.

Sweetness is what got the apple out of the Kazakh forests, across Europe, to the shores of North America, and eventually into John Chapman's canoe. But the appeal of apples goes beyond their taste. They are "sweet" in the broader sense of the word.

To European colonists in the New World, like the New England Puritans, fruit trees represented home, good fortune, and stability.

There was also the fact that the apple was believed to be the tree Adam and Eve ate from in the Garden of Eden. Never mind that the Bible doesn't name the tree or the fruit. Or the fact that the Middle East is generally too hot for apple trees. The apple managed to "worm" its way into the biblical story, especially after countless artists painted it there. The Puritans who colonized New England thought that their settlement would be a new "promised land," a second Eden. They needed apple trees to complete that picture. That may be the reason that the New England Puritans gave cider a pass. The Bible warns against wine but says nothing about cider.

Appleseed Country

I picked up the trail of Johnny Appleseed again in Mount Vernon, Ohio. Even today the place has the outline of a classic early American town. A modest grid of streets is laid out around a central square of green that is a short walk from the meeting place of two streams. In the library on the square is a map of the town made in 1805, the year it was founded.

If you look down in the bottom left-hand corner of the map, next to Owl Creek, you can see lots 145 and 147, both of which were bought by John Chapman in 1809 for the sum of fifty dollars. Follow the creek to the far right-hand edge of the map, and you'll see a drawing of a neat row of apple trees. That picture represents what is thought to be one of Chapman's nurseries.

I'd come to Mount Vernon to meet Ohio's leading authority on Johnny Appleseed, a man named William Ellery Jones. When I had phoned him the month before at his home in Cincinnati, he generously offered to give me a guided tour of "Johnny Appleseed country." He's a tall, elegant man with pale blue eyes who gives the impression of being somewhat out of place in time. He's also deeply devoted to the classic story of Johnny Appleseed. To Jones, that story represents a simpler, better America. I got the feeling he chose to overlook the parts of the story he didn't like.

In Mount Vernon, Jones took me on a brisk morning walk to plots 145 and 147 on the banks of Owl Creek. Chapman's Mount Vernon property was, I would discover, typical of his holdings. The land hugged a stream, ensuring water for his seedlings and sales traffic later, and the plots were located on the edge of a new town. Today they stand across the street from each other and are paved over as parking lots for an auto tire store. Owl Creek looked shallow and sluggish, but Jones pointed out that reservoirs and dams had long ago tamed most of the local streams and rivers.

Over the next few days Jones showed me a dozen of Chapman's former nurseries. On the banks of the Auglaize River, we found the site of the famous sycamore tree stump where Chapman had once spent a winter. It is now on the front lawn of a ranch house. In a run-down section of Mansfield, we visited the site of the home of Chapman's kid sister, a woman named Persis Broom. Today the lot is occupied by a drive-through liquor store called the Galloping Goose. In Defiance, Ohio, we climbed to the top of a water treatment plant to get an unobstructed view of one Appleseed nursery, and near Loudonville we paddled a canoe for two hours to catch a glimpse of another. On a farm outside Savannah, we took pictures of each other standing next to an ancient, half-dead apple tree that may or may not have been planted by Chapman.

All the while Jones told me tales of Johnny Appleseed, a rich soup of legend sprinkled with chunks of fact. Most of what's known about Chapman comes from accounts left by the many settlers who welcomed him into their cabins. They seem to have been glad to have a guest who was literally a legend in his own time. In exchange for a meal and a place to sleep he shared news from his travels and stories of his latest deeds. And of course, Chapman would usually plant a couple of apple trees as a token of thanks.

It was clear that Chapman lived everywhere and nowhere. He was constantly on the move, traveling in autumn to Pennsylvania to gather seeds, scouting nursery sites and planting in spring, repairing fences at old nurseries in summer. Wherever he planted, he signed up local agents to keep an eye on and sell his trees. Even into his sixties, after moving his base of operations to Indiana, Chapman made an annual pilgrimage to central Ohio to look after his nurseries there. Despite his loose business arrangements, he managed to buy considerable property. And he had enough money to give away to people in need, frequently strangers.

One morning, Jones and I set out to canoe a stretch of the Mohican River north of Loudonville. He wanted to show me a riverside nursery of Chapman's, and I was curious to see the country from the water. That would have been how Chapman usually saw it. For both the Native Americans and the white settlers, rivers were often the best and easiest way to get around.

The sun was not yet up over the trees when we put into the river a few miles above Perrysville. I took the seat up front since Jones was the more experienced canoer. The water looked like a freshly blacktopped road. In places spooky mists rose from the surface, and the banks were thickly lined with trees. Giant cottonwoods and twisted sycamores leaned way out over the water. It wasn't hard to pretend we were back in 1806. We slipped by ducks and saw a woodpecker hammering the trunk of a dead tree.

After we'd been paddling along for an hour or so, Jones pointed to a broad table of open land off to our left. This was the site of Greentown, a sprawling village of the Delaware people that Chapman often visited. It was torched by white settlers during the War of 1812 when many of the Native American tribes took the side of the British. Just a few hundred yards farther on, at the spot where a tiny creek dribbled into the river, was the site of Chapman's apple tree nursery. I lifted my paddle, and through the trees I could see a rough stubble of corn on a gently curving skin of earth.

Chapman moved easily between the white farmers and Native Americans, even when the two were at war. The Native Americans respected Chapman as a brilliant woodsman and medicine man. In addition to the apples, Chapman brought with him the seeds of a dozen different medicinal plants, including mullein, motherwort, dandelion, wintergreen, pennyroyal, and mayweed, and he was expert in their use.

This was one of Chapman's many contradictions. He was friendly with Native Americans, yet in the War of 1812, he helped the settlers by running messages for them. He was an expert backwoodsman, yet a capable businessman. He loved nature, yet he helped the settlers to move in and remake the landscape. He could look like a barefoot wild man yet could talk for hours about Swedenborgian religious beliefs.

When I got home from my trip to Ohio, I tried to get a clear picture of John Chapman, but the contradictions kept getting in the way. I compared the legends, the cleaned-up story of Chapman, and what I knew to be the facts of this very unusual person. If I looked at him from the point of view of his fellow colonists, then the real Johnny Appleseed was a very clever, very odd human with a strong love and attachment to nature. But looking at him from the point of view of his beloved apple trees, I saw a different picture. For John Chapman was a perfect living example of the great partnership between plants and people.

The European colonists remade the land to fit their image. They brought with them the plants and animals they were accustomed to back in Europe. They cut down forests, and planted the grasses their livestock needed to thrive and the herbs to keep themselves healthy. They set out gardens of Old World fruits and flowers to make life comfortable. But they weren't aware of some of the changes they made. In addition to the seeds they wanted to grow, they also brought along seeds of less desirable plants. These stowaways hid in the cracks of their boots or the feed bags of their horses. They also brought new microbes and diseases to the New World.

Those colonists saw the plants and animals they brought as their tools and servants. But John Chapman treated his apple seeds and trees as his equal. His decision to not graft but plant millions of seeds was a fateful one. It allowed the apple to adapt to its new home. By letting the apple do its thing and reproduce an astonishing variety of trees, he allowed it to evolve. That gave the apple the opportunity to discover by trial and error the precise combination of traits required to prosper in the New World. From Chapman's vast planting of nameless cider apple seeds came some of the great American apples of the nineteenth century.

You could say Chapman had faith in the apple and in nature. John Chapman's millions of seeds and thousands of miles changed the apple, and the apple took its place in American history and culture. For that, Johnny Appleseed deserves his place in our history.

The Great Apple Rush

As far as I know, John Chapman never set foot in Geneva, New York, but there is an orchard there I think he would have loved. On the banks of Seneca Lake, in excellent apple-growing country, is a government agency called the Plant Genetic Resources Unit. It maintains the world's largest collection of apple trees. Some 2,500 different varieties have been gathered from all over the world. They are planted in pairs, as if on a beached botanical ark.

A few weeks after my trip to the Midwest, I traveled there, to see what of Johnny Appleseed's legacy I might find. At first glance the orchard looks much like any other, with tidy rows of grafted trees advancing in straight lines to the horizon. But it doesn't take long before you begin to notice the stupendous variety—in color, leaf, and shape.

When I visited, it was late October, and most of the trees were bent with ripe fruit. Some had already dropped a carpet of red and yellow and green apples on the ground. I spent the better part of a morning browsing the leafy aisles, tasting all the famous old varieties I'd read about—the Esopus Spitzenburg and Newtown Pippin, the Hawkeye and the Winter Banana. Almost all of these classic apples began as seedlings found in exactly the sort of cider orchards John Chapman planted. No doubt there were some that came from seeds planted by Chapman himself. There's just no way of knowing which ones they are.

As I worked my way up and down the aisles, I consulted a computerized directory that the collection's curator, Phil Forsline, had printed out for me. The card catalog of this fifty-acre tree archive includes strange varieties like Adam's Pearmain, an antique English apple, and the German Zucalmagio. I concentrated on the varieties listed as "American" and thought about exactly what that meant. By planting so many apples from seed, Americans like Chapman had conducted a vast evolutionary experiment. They allowed the Old World apple to try out literally millions of new genetic combinations, allowing it to adapt to its new life in America.

Many of the seeds failed to grow or thrive in American soil. Many others were killed off by harsh American winters. A freeze in May killed off buds on some other trees, preventing them from putting out fruit and new seeds. The ones that survived and grew fruit were ever so slightly more American. When their seeds were planted, the great contest began again. The winners would thrive on American soil.

Of course, humans didn't just sit back and watch. Every now and then, they would discover a random tree growing in the middle of a cider orchard. This genetic accident might be especially hardy, or its fruit might be tasty and sweet instead of bitter, or it might have a pleasing red color. Then the orchard owner would promptly make a cutting and graft it onto a rootstock, reproducing that exact variety of apple.

The owner of this genetic winner would also give it a name, such as Jonathan or Baldwin or Grimes Golden. This early example of branding was important, because a new, desirable apple variety could mean a fortune to the person who owned and grafted it.

In the years after John Chapman began his travels, America witnessed what has sometimes been called the Great Apple Rush. People searched the countryside for the next champion fruit. The discovery of a popular apple could bring wealth and even a measure of fame. Every farmer tended their cider orchard with an eye to discovering the next apple that would hit it big. The odds of finding a good eating apple were commonly thought to be eighty thousand to one. Finding one would be like winning the lottery.

The nationwide hunt for a better apple brought forth literally hundreds of new varieties. The orchard in Geneva holds many of them. I can report, however, that not all these children of Chapman are outstanding to eat. Many of the apples I sampled that morning were spitters. The Wolf River is particularly memorable in this respect. It had yellow, wet sawdust flesh and not a hint of red beauty.

Beyond Red Delicious

As I sampled them, I marveled at the sheer number of types of apples. This will come as a surprise to most of us. Our supermarkets carry Gala, Honeycrisp, Red Delicious, Macintosh, Granny Smith, Fuji, and at most two or three others. Perhaps if you go to a farmer's market, you might find one or two so-called heritage apples. But at the Plant Genetic Resources Unit, I found apples that barely resembled any of those, in color, size, shape, or taste.

There were apples that tasted like bananas, others like pears. I tasted spicy apples and sticky-sweet ones, apples tart and fresh as lemons and others rich as nuts. I picked apples that weighed more than a pound, others small enough to fit in a toddler's pocket. I saw yellow apples, green apples, spotted apples, tan apples, striped apples, purple apples, even a near-blue apple. There were apples with a natural polished sheen and apples that wore a dusty bloom on their cheeks.

Many of these varieties have special qualities that go beyond taste. There are apples that taste sweeter in March than October. There are some that make especially good cider or preserves or apple butter. Some could last half a year in storage without refrigeration. Some varieties produce apples that ripen at staggered times. That's helpful if you don't want too many apples at once. But then there are some whose apples ripen all at once. That's helpful if you only want to harvest them in a short period of time.

There are apples with long stems or short, thin skin or thick, apples that will taste wonderful only if grown in Virginia and others that needed a hard New England frost to reach perfection. There are apples that redden in August, others that hold off till winter. There were even apples that could sit at the bottom of a barrel for the six weeks it took a ship to get to Europe, then emerge bright and crisp enough to command a top price in London.

And the names these apples had! Names that reek of the

American nineteenth century. I could imagine these names coming out of the mouth of an old-time carnival barker, or a proud mayor of some tiny rural hamlet. There were the names that simply described, like the green-as-a-bottle Bottle Greening. Also, there were the Sheepnose, the Oxheart Pippin, the Yellow Bellflower, the Black Gilliflower, the Twenty-Ounce Pippin. There were the names that puffed with hometown pride, like the Westfield Seek-No-Further, the Hubbardston Nonesuch, the Rhode Island Greening, the Albemarle Pippin, the York Imperial, the Kentucky Redstreak, the Long Stem of Pennsylvania, the Ladies Favorite of Tennessee, the King of Tompkins County, and the Peach of Kentucky.

Some proud orchard owners gave their own names to their apples. These include the Baldwin, the Macintosh, the Jonathan, McAfee's Red, Norton's Melon, Moyer's Prize, Metzger's Calville, Kelly's White, and Walker's Beauty. And then there were the names that denoted an apple's specialty, like Wismer's Dessert, Jacob's Sweet Winter, the Early Harvest and Cider Apple, the Clothes-Yard Apple, Cornell's Savewell, Payne's Late Keeper, and Hay's Winter Wine. There is even one that tells you what it should be served with: the Bread and Cheese.

How many other fruits do we call by their names? There are a few named pears and a famous peach or two. Still, no other fruit in history has produced so many household names and celebrities. Like sports teams or pop stars, each had its group of supporters. Some proud owners even erected monuments to mark the spot where that apple had first appeared on a tree.

Like superheroes, many had their own origin stories. The Baldwin, it is said, was discovered by a surveyor who stumbled on a tree growing by a Boston canal. The York Imperial was discovered by a farmer who noticed the neighborhood children drawn each fall to the apples of one special tree.

And then there was the stubborn, possibly miraculous seedling that kept coming up in between the rows of Jesse Hiatt's orchard in Peru, Iowa. The little tree kept coming back no matter how many times the farmer mowed it down. Finally, the farmer decided to let the tree grow big enough to have fruit, only to discover its apples were far and away the best he'd ever tasted. Hiatt named it the Hawkeye and in 1893 shipped four apples to a contest at the Stark Brothers Nurseries in Louisiana, Missouri. They won first prize and were awarded a shiny new name: the Delicious.

Alas, Jesse Hiatt's entry card was somehow misplaced, setting off a frantic yearlong search for what would eventually become the world's most popular apple. Today a granite monument marks the spot where the original Red Delicious grew between the rows on Jesse Hiatt's Iowa farm.

A Democratic Fruit

There were dozens of apple stories like this, rags-to-riches fables linking a wonderful fruit tree to a particular American person and place. These stories seemed to prove that even a lowly farmer, who kept his eyes open (and had a little bit of luck) could strike it rich. In this way, the apple became a bright symbol of the American dream.

A great apple is (or was) something that arrived by chance. It just happened. This set it apart from many other plants that people valued. A great rose, for example, is the result of careful breeding, the deliberate crossing of already great parents. Rose breeders call these valued roses "elite lines." They are the aristocrats of roses. But a great apple didn't need elite parents. It could be discovered by anyone, rich or poor. Any seedling had a chance to grow up to be a famous apple preferred by millions. This is one reason the apple was referred to as the "democratic fruit."

Today the arrival of new apple varieties is no longer left to chance. Botanists use careful cross-pollination to combine traits from existing types to create new hybrids. But in the 1800s the history of the apple was a history of heroic individuals. There was only a single Golden Delicious tree that stood until the 1950s on a hillside in Clay County, West Virginia, where it lived inside a padlocked steel cage wired with a burglar alarm. Every tree bearing that name is a grafted clone of the original.

These successful apples were produced naturally through long trial and error. They are the result of literally millions of apple seeds, each one genetically different, each set out in American soil to thrive or die. The ones that thrived are uniquely American, adapted to the soil and climate. Some have since found homes in distant lands (the Golden Delicious now grows on five continents). But many others can only live on this continent. In some cases, they're adapted to life in a single region.

The Jonathan, for example, does best in the American Midwest (which is somewhat surprising, considering it was discovered in the Hudson Valley). My guess is that the Jonathan would be as out of place in England or Kazakhstan, the native ground of its ancestors, as I would be in Russia, the native ground of my own. At this point, the Jonathan's as much an American as I am.

Beyond Red Delicious

The golden age of American apples lives on in the Geneva orchard—yet just about no place else. The job of the Plant Genetic Resources Unit is to preserve these old apple varieties. Many have already been allowed to disappear. They were ignored and then forgotten by an industry that found it easier to grow and market just a few types. As a result, the apples you can buy today present us with a very narrow idea of what sweetness tastes like and what an apple should be.

The first great cut in our roster of apples happened when the temperance movement literally cut down the American cider orchard. Those wild, ungrafted trees grown from seed were the source of large-scale genetic experimentation. Thanks to temperance, and then Prohibition, Americans were told to stop drinking apples as cider and to eat them instead. This meant most apple growers had to start grafting apple trees, to get fruit that people would want to eat.

Around the same time, refrigeration made possible a national market for apples. Fruit grown in Washington State could be shipped and sold in New York. But to simplify their shipping and marketing, the growers decided to only plant and promote a small handful of brand-name varieties. Those brand names had to be easy to sell, and so they had to have just two simple, easy to recognize qualities. They had to be bright red, and they had to be very sweet.

There was no room for anything else in the new marketplace. Many of the famous apples of the nineteenth century just didn't fit this new model. If they weren't red and shiny, it didn't matter how good they tasted, they were no longer planted. And they couldn't be anything but sweet. The old-style apples, even when they were sweet, had a touch of acid or bite to them. Sweetness in an apple now meant sugariness, plain and simple.

That's how the Red Delicious came to dominate the American orchard. It has a pure, sweet taste and a beautiful red skin that can be polished to a dazzling shine. The one exception to the red and sweet rule is the Granny Smith, a relatively tart green apple discovered in Australia in 1868 (by a Mrs. Smith). It survives in part because of its usefulness in cooking and its beautiful green skin. It's also virtually indestructible in shipping.

Today apple breeders are locked in a kind of sweetness battle with junk food. The apple has to compete in a culture where sugar is becoming cheap and plentiful. It has to fight for shelf space with hundreds of sugary snack foods. And so when developing new apples, growers lean heavily on the genes of the very sweet Red Delicious and the unrelated Yellow Delicious. Most of the popular apples developed in the last few years, including the Fuji and the Gala, are hybrids or mixes of the Delicious and its offspring. Thousands of apple traits, and the genes that code those traits, have become extinct.

That's why the Geneva orchard is a kind of apple bank. Its curator, Phil Forsline, explained it to me.

"Today's commercial apples represent only a small fraction of the apple gene pool," he said. "A century ago, there were several thousand different varieties of apples being sold. Now most of the apples we grow have the same five parents: Red Delicious, Golden Delicious, Jonathan, Macintosh, and Cox's Orange Pippin."

Forsline led me to a far corner of the orchard where there was something he wanted me to see. He's a tall, wiry man with striking Nordic blue eyes and sandy hair starting to gray. He's devoted his career to preserving and expanding the apple's genetic diversity. He's convinced that the modern history of the apple has made it less fit as a plant.

That is, he says, one reason modern apples require more pesticide than any other food crop. When apple trees were grown from seed, the trees were able to evolve and keep pace with threats like insects and disease. As we've seen, the trial and error of producing thousands of different varieties meant that some emerge that are better suited to the climate, soil, and local pests.

Today, with trees reproduced through grafting, apple growers have stopped the natural process of evolution. But viruses, bacteria, fungi, and insects haven't stopped evolving. Like wild apple trees, they do this through sexual reproduction, which simply means combining genes from two parents. This is the trial and error of evolution. While grafted apple trees are frozen with one set of genes, their enemies continue to try new combinations, and sooner or later, they evolve and can overcome whatever resistance the apple trees have. Suddenly the pests have a new advantage, and the apple trees, held back from evolving new defenses, are at their mercy.

Modern farmers make up for this by using chemistry to produce stronger pesticides (which get sprayed on our food). Of course, the insects and other pests continue to evolve until the pesticides no longer work. Then the scientists go back to the lab to make new pesticides, and so on. (This is not true for organic apples, which are grown without the use of artificial, industrial pesticides.)

"The solution is for us to help the apple evolve artificially," Forsline explained as we walked down the long rows of antique apples, tasting as we talked.

Artificial evolution is done by breeding new types of apples through cross-pollination. This is the same way that the Fuji and Gala apples were produced. But to produce a better apple, we need to use more than five or six varieties as our source. And we need to be looking at qualities beyond sweetness and redness. The orchard Forsline watches over contains thousands of those possibilities—it's a storehouse of apple biodiversity.

I was accustomed to thinking of biodiversity in terms of wild species. When a species of frog or bird becomes extinct, we say there has been a reduction in biodiversity. Also, when a population of wild animals becomes too small, they also suffer from a lack of biodiversity. As a group, they have a smaller pool of genes or possibilities to pass on to their offspring. That makes it harder for them to evolve and adapt.

But biodiversity is also important for the domesticated species on which we depend—and which now depend on us. This is true for animals like chickens and cows. It's also true for plants like corn, potatoes, and apples. Every time an old apple variety is allowed to disappear, a set of genes—which is to say a set of qualities of taste and color and resistance to pests—vanishes from the earth. We need those genes to help our domesticated partners meet the challenges they face.

Apple Preserves

The greatest biodiversity of any species is typically found in the place where it first evolved. That is where nature first experimented with all the possibilities of what an apple, or a potato or peach, could be. In the case of the apple, the center of diversity lies in Kazakhstan. In the last few years, Forsline and his colleagues set out to preserve as many of those wild apple genes as they could. They made several trips to Asia, bringing back thousands of seeds and cuttings that they planted in two long rows all the way in the back of the Geneva orchard. It was these trees, apples far older and wilder than any planted by Johnny Appleseed, that Forsline wanted to show me.

Nikolai Vavilov, a great Russian botanist, was the one who

first identified the wild apple's home in the forests around Almaty, Kazakhstan. This wouldn't have come as news to the locals, however: *Almaty* means "father of the apple."

"All around the city one could see a vast expanse of wild apples covering the foothills," Vavilov wrote in 1929. "One could see with his own eyes that this beautiful site was the origin of the cultivated apple."

Vavilov eventually fell victim to the dictatorship of the Soviet Union. Under that system, science didn't matter as much as politics. Scientists were expected to go along with whatever the communists wanted them to say, whether it was true or not. Vavilov died in prison and his discovery of the apple's origin was lost until the fall of communism.

But one of Vavilov's students, a botanist named Aimak Djangaliev, quietly continued to study the wild apples of Almaty. In 1989 he invited a group of American botanists to visit. Djangaliev was already eighty, and he wanted the Americans' help to save the wild apple forests from a wave of real estate development spreading out from Almaty to the surrounding hills.

Forsline and his colleagues were astonished to find entire forests of apples. There were three-hundred-year-old trees fifty feet tall and as big around as oaks. Some of them were bearing apples as large and red as modern cultivated varieties.

"Even in the towns, apple trees were coming up in the cracks of the sidewalks," Forsline recalled. "You looked at these apples and felt sure you were looking at the ancestor of the Golden Delicious or the Macintosh."

Forsline was determined to save as much of this apple genetic diversity as possible. He felt certain that somewhere among the wild apples of Kazakhstan could be found genes for disease and pest resistance, as well as apple qualities beyond our imagining. Since the wild apple's survival in the wild was now in doubt, he collected hundreds of thousands of seeds, planted as many as he had space for in Geneva, and then offered the rest to researchers and breeders around the world. "I'll send seeds to anybody who asks, just so long as they promise to plant them, tend to the trees, and then report back someday." The wild apples had found a new Johnny Appleseed.

We got to the edge of the orchard and there they were, two wildly jumbled rows of the weirdest apples I'd ever laid eyes on. The trees had been crammed in next to one another. The rows could barely contain the riot of foliage and fruit, even though they had been planted only six years before. Forsline had told me that all the apple genes brought to America by European colonists—all the genes floating down the Ohio River alongside John Chapman—represented maybe a tenth of what existed in the wild. Here was a sample of the rest of it.

No two of these trees looked even remotely alike, not in form or leaf or fruit. Some grew straight for the sun, others trailed along the ground or formed low shrubs. Some simply petered out, the Upstate New York climate not to their liking. I saw trees with leaves of every shape. Maybe a third of the trees were bearing fruit—but strange, strange fruit that looked and tasted like God's first drafts of what an apple could be.

I saw apples with the color and weight of olives and some that looked like cherries. They grew alongside trees with glowing yellow Ping-Pong balls and others with dusky purple berries. I saw a whole assortment of baseballs, some flattened, some cone shaped, and some perfectly round. Some of them were as bright as infield grass, others dull as wood. And I picked big, shiny red fruits that looked just like apples, though their taste was something else again. Imagine sinking your teeth into a tart potato or a slightly mushy Brazil nut covered in leather. On first bite some of these apples would start out with a promise of sweetness only to suddenly turn so bitter, just the memory of it makes my stomach rise.

To get the taste off my tongue, I made for a more civilized row nearby and picked something edible—a Jonagold, a cross, or hybrid, of Golden Delicious and Jonathan. That apple is to my thinking one of the great achievements of modern apple breeding. And what an achievement it is, a delight to the eye and tongue. This whole orchard is proof of the magic arts of domestication, and of the unique partnership between humans and the apple.

That partnership has been so successful because the apple has offered humans so many possible versions of itself. Over and over, through the random combination of genes, the apple produced new variations. When it hit on one humans liked, we took it and spread it far and wide.

Johnny Appleseed and the cider growers allowed that genetic diversity to flourish. But the modern apple growers have worked against diversity. We have domesticated our apple partner to the point where it cannot evolve on its own. By limiting our partner, we've greatly weakened it.

The Treasure of Wildness

Something like that happened to the potato in Ireland in the 1840s. The potato (which we will visit in a later chapter) came from the Andes Mountains in South America. It was brought back to Europe by the Spanish conquerors of the Americas, but it wasn't until it landed in Ireland that it became widely adopted. By the 1840s the potato was an essential part of the Irish diet. Then in 1845, a disease, a fungus called the potato blight, struck. Potatoes across the country rotted in heaps. The result was widespread hunger and death.

The potatoes grown in Ireland at that time were of only one variety. That variety grew very well in the Irish climate, but it had no resistance to the blight. This meant disaster for millions of Irish people who had no other source of food. Yet at that same moment, thousands of miles away, there were potatoes growing that could resist the fungus of the blight. They were growing back in the Andes, the home of the potato. Like Kazakhstan for the apple, the Andes are the center of potato biodiversity. Since then, scientists have used genes from those ancient potatoes to breed potatoes that can resist the blight.

We live in a world where the wild places are dwindling.

What happens if we let the wild potatoes and wild apples disappear? The best technology in the world can't create a new gene or re-create one that's been lost. That's why Phil Forsline has dedicated himself to saving and spreading all manner of apples. He knows it doesn't matter how they taste or what they look like. Each variety that survives could hold a treasure like resistance to disease or a new, amazing taste.

Domesticated plants and animals represent only a tiny fraction of what exists in the wild. The handful of apple varieties we grow are an even tinier fraction of the wild apples that once existed. We are learning, hopefully before it's too late, that the wilderness isn't something to be tamed and paved over. It's a source of beauty and biodiversity that, if it's allowed to disappear, can never be replaced.

A handful of wild apples came home with me from Geneva, a couple of big red ones that caught my eye and a tiny round one no bigger than an olive. This last oddball sat on my desk for a few weeks. When it started to wrinkle, I sliced it through with a knife and scratched out the five seeds inside. Those seeds held a mystery. There was no way of knowing what sort of apple would come of such seeds, or of *their* seeds in turn.

If I planted them and the trees survived and put forth flowers, the bees in my garden would go to work. They'd mix the pollen from the new trees with the Baldwins and Macintosh in my garden. What kind of apple would come of that genetic mixing? Probably not one you'd want to eat or even look at. But who can say for sure? I decided to give one of the wild apple seeds a spot in my garden anyway—in honor of John Chapman, I suppose, but also just to see what happened.

Though it may not be realistic to expect a sweet apple ever to come of a wildling, I would be surprised if it didn't add something to my garden. Even if the apples aren't sweet, I think the tree will make the garden a sweeter place than it is now. That is, sweeter in the sense of good or even perfect. Imagine it, a strangely formed tree growing up in a garden, an apple tree like no apple ever seen. In the fall it would bear a harvest of strange fruits you might not even recognize.

That wild tree growing in the middle of my tamed, ordered garden is a living symbol of the way we humans live in partnership with the natural world, whether we know it or not. It will be a reminder to me that though I think I'm in charge, like all of us, I depend on our plant and animal partners to survive. And though they may be domesticated, it's their wild heritage that makes them such good partners.

My garden is bordered by a dwindling row of ancient, twisted Baldwin apple trees. They were planted in the 1920s by a farmer who, local legend has it, made the apples into the tastiest applejack in town. My wild Kazakh apple tree will grow up in the middle of its named and cultivated descendants. I think it will make those old Baldwins taste sweeter because it will remind me of all the generations of people and apples that came before. And if I ever do get around to making a barrel of cider from my Baldwins, I'll be sure to add a few of the ancient wild apples in memory of John Chapman and the cider orchards of the past.

Chapter Two

Desire: *Beauty*

Plant: *The Tulip*

The tulip was the first flower I ever planted. Every

fall my parents would buy mesh bags of tulip bulbs, twenty-five or fifty to the bag. Then they'd pay me a few pennies per bulb to plant them in the border of our lawn. I think they were after a kind of woodsy effect, with the flowers growing as if they'd been scattered naturally. That's why they were happy to have a ten-year-old do the job. My work would never be too neat or orderly.

I used a bulb planter, a handheld tool sort of like a cookie cutter that carves a round hole in the dirt. I'd press it and twist it into hard earth, cutting a nice round hole. Then I dropped one bulb in the hole, narrow end up, and covered it over with dirt. I did this until the heel of my hand was covered with a large blister, keeping careful count of each bulb I planted, thinking of each one as one more piece of candy or pack of baseball cards. I definitely wasn't thinking about the colorful show the bulbs would put on in the spring.

Every year, my blisters in October brought forth the first real color of spring. The daffodils came first, but to me those yellow blooms hardly counted. Tulips, on the other hand, came in many other colors besides yellow: red, pink, orange, or purple. Those were the colors that attracted my eye. And since it was the early days of the space program, the tulip stalks reminded me of rockets ready for launch.

The tulips I planted were the type that were very popular in the 1950s and '60s. They were simple, with each stalk producing one big, bright, solid-colored flower. When they came up, it was like a box of crayons had bloomed. They were easy to understand, easy to draw, and also, for me anyway, easy to forget.

Later, when I had a garden of my own, I had no time for

tulips. My parents let me use a narrow bed along the foundation of our house as my own. In that small plot, I could plant whatever I wanted, and I certainly didn't want flowers. For me, fruits and vegetables were the only things worth growing, even vegetables you couldn't pay me to eat. I thought of myself as a farmer, transforming seeds, soil, water, and sunlight into things of value.

I suppose if I could have grown toys or records, I would have grown those. But since that wasn't possible, growing groceries was a way to produce something practical and useful. I even had my own farm stand, though my mother was my only customer.

Then and now, I was attracted to the beauty of the fruits of my garden: a glossy green bell pepper ready to be picked and eaten, or a ripe watermelon nestled in a tangle of vines. Of course, all fruits begin as flowers, and I understood that. I liked seeing the yellow trumpet on a zucchini vine, because I knew it would grow into a zucchini. The pretty white-and-yellow button of a strawberry blossom would swell and redden and become a strawberry.

The Gift of Beauty

I now know that the vegetables had evolved a way to get me to plant and tend them. They offered me food in return for my hard work. But at that age I just couldn't see, or appreciate, what the tulip was offering—a chance to enjoy beauty.

This is an offer that humans have accepted for centuries. Many people's gardens are filled with purely ornamental flowers, ones that will never bear edible fruit—roses, peonies, daisies, and hundreds more varieties. Those plants have developed a different way to get people to grow them. They don't appeal to our taste buds and our stomachs. They appeal to our senses of sight and smell.

That appeal can be very powerful. More than three hundred years ago, the beauty of tulips shook an entire nation. From 1633 to 1637, the country of Holland was captured by "tulipomania." People went crazy buying tulip bulbs, driving up prices until a single bulb was sold for an amount that would have bought one of the grandest canal houses in Amsterdam. Of course, much of the mania was driven by the chance to make a fortune *selling* tulip bulbs. But the market for the bulbs only existed because the tulip plant offered beauty to humans.

Producing beauty is an evolutionary strategy that's proven every bit as effective as producing sweetness. But beauty, unlike the sweetness of an apple, is much harder to define. In this chapter I explore how flowers came to this strategy, and why it works on so many people (though not some ten-year-olds). I've chosen to focus on the tulip, both because of its place in my personal history and because its story is truly amazing.

Throughout history, in most cultures around the world, people have been attracted to the beauty of flowers. In ancient Egypt, the dead were buried with flowers to take with them on their journey to the afterlife. Some of these blooms have been found in the pyramids, miraculously preserved. There's evidence that even earlier—70,000 years ago—the Neanderthals, cousins of modern humans, also buried their dead with flowers.

From those ancient roots, the partnership between flow-ers and humans has grown around the world. What is the basis of that partnership? What is it about these plant reproductive organs (that's what they are) that appeals to us? Why do we think they're beautiful?

A Call for Help

We saw that apples and other fruiting plants produce food to lure animals into eating and spreading their seeds. That also works with humans. We want the food the plants produce and in return we help the plants reproduce. (Though we don't spread the seeds the same way animals do!)

All fruits and seeds start out as flowers. So do tree nuts. (By the way, "fruits" includes things we often call vegetables, like tomatoes and bell peppers. Anything with seeds in it is techni-cally a fruit.) Flowers evolved to get insects like bees to help them reproduce. They do so by pollinating the plant, which simply means they spread the pollen produced inside the flower. Besides bees, other insects like wasps and animals like hummingbirds are also pollinators.

Pollen holds the male reproductive DNA of the plant. It is produced and held by structures in the flower called stamen. The pistil is the ovary of the flower and holds the female reproduc-tive DNA, or *ovules* (eggs). Pollinators are attracted to flowers by the sweet nectar inside. They fly from flower to flower, drinking nectar and spreading pollen. They pick up the pollen by brushing against the stamen.

When a grain of pollen lands on a pistil, it travels down into the ovary and joins with an ovule. The ovule then starts to grow into a seed that contains a tiny plant embryo. The rest of the pistil grows into a piece of fruit. Every piece of fruit started out as a flower. Apples start as apple blossoms. Sometimes if you look at the bottom of an apple before you eat it, you can see the tiny remains of the stamen, called a calyx.

All of this is a form of sexual reproduction that simply means every offspring has genes from two parents. Some plants have flowers that are only male (with stamen) or female (with pistils). Many flowers have both. But many flowers have evolved to make sure that they don't fertilize themselves so their offspring get genes from two different parents. They avoid self-pollination in several ways. In some plants the pollen simply can't mate with its own ovule. In others, the stamen and pistil in the flower are spaced to avoid contact. Or the pollen and ovule might develop at different times.

Flowers are the way plants advertise to pollinators. Their colors, shapes, and scents (beside the scent of nectar) have evolved to tell pollinators to "come and get it." In a way, a flower is a call for help, or an offer of partnership. They say, "Come and spread my pollen and you can get a drink of nectar."

But we humans, unlike bees or hummingbirds, are not natural pollinators. We don't drink nectar, yet we are also attracted to the colors and smells of flowers. Why should that be? Why should those lures that evolved to attract insects and birds work on us? Why aren't most people like I was as a ten-year-old? Why do we even notice flowers?

You might think, "Because they're beautiful," but that doesn't really answer the question. Why do we find them beautiful? Why do so many people spend time and money to grow flowers and not, say, pinecones or moss? Today we have thousands of varieties of flowers that have been bred to be pleasing to people, either through color or scent, or both. But ancient tombs prove that thousands of years ago, before we began changing them, people already thought flowers were beautiful. There had to be something about them that drew our attention, some reason people needed them for survival.

The Language of Flowers

One theory is that early humans (and our nonhuman ancestors) were like I was as a child. They knew, as I did, that flowers became food. Early humans who paid attention to flowers were able to predict where food would appear. This gave them a big advantage, for if they remembered the spot, they could return just as the fruit ripened before any other animals (or other humans) could get there. Of course, they'd have to learn which flowers became fruit that was good to eat, and exactly when to return when the fruit would be ready.

We evolved to love and seek out sweetness because it signaled a good food source. (This is a problem today when sugar is cheap and plentiful.) It's possible that we may have evolved to love flowers because they represent the promise of food. That may have caused us to think of flowers as beautiful even when, like the tulip, they don't produce food for us. (On the other hand, deer love to eat them.)

Perhaps this is one reason flowers often make us think of the passing of time. We know they are around only briefly. This is a good thing if you're hoping to harvest fruit, but it also can carry a bit of sadness. Faded flowers are a strong symbol of loss and regret. The fact that they soon wither may add to their beauty, for we know we have only a short time to enjoy them.

Whatever the original reason, flowers have long held a special place in our imaginations. Think of all the poems, songs, paintings, and other works of art that have flowers as their subject. Flowers can represent love or happiness, grief or loss. In some cultures, flowers have been used to send coded messages. This is the so-called language of flowers, in which each type of bloom has its own meaning. These can be very specific. For example, in England in the 1800s, a daisy meant loyalty, but a marigold meant grief.

This shouldn't surprise us, for sending messages is what evolution has designed flowers to do. Their whole purpose is to communicate with other species. To do this, they use an astonishing number of ways to get the attention of specific insects and animals.

Some plants go so far as to impersonate other creatures or things. Carnivorous plants eat insects or even small animals, but like all plants, they can't move and so can't hunt. They have instead evolved ways to get their prey to come to them. Pitcher plants have weirdly shaped maroon-and-white flowers that look and smell like rotting meat. To some flies, this combination is like a dinner bell. They fly into the plant looking for a meal, get trapped, and then become a meal themselves.

Ophrys orchids have evolved to look like insects, either bees or flies. In this way, they attract male insects looking for a mate. The insects fly in and pollinate the orchid and they don't even get a drink of nectar in return.

The Crowded Garden

Every summer my own garden offers proof that flowers are masters of communication. In the middle of July, the place is crowded with flowers. At first glance it can be a confusing mix of color and scent with a soundtrack of buzzing insects and rustling leaves. It's a place thick with information, almost like Times Square with flashing lights and signs in every direction. But take a moment to look carefully and individual flowers begin to come into focus.

Start with the roses. By July they are almost finished, leaving behind mostly bare shrubs stuck with sad bits of withered blooms. But some varieties, like the rugosas and teas are still pumping out color, attracting attention. Tangled up in the petals, the Japanese beetles are dining intently.

Farther down the path the daylilies lean forward expectantly, waiting. If you look closely, you can see tiny wasps climb way up into their throats in search of nectar. The sugar almost makes them drunk by the time they crawl out. Before they do, they jostle the lily's stamens, coating themselves with pollen they'll later dust off on the pistils of some other blossom.

At the front of the bed the flowers called lamb's ears form a low, soft, gray forest. The leaves seem like they're coated in gray wool, which is how they got their name. The tall flower spikes that shoot up from the gray leaves look as though they've been dipped into a vat of bees. Each spike is completely covered, a crowd of wings making the whole flower vibrate with the motion of the insects. Above them the plume poppies have put out clouds of tiny white flowers, which are also irresistible to honeybees, who swim in the air among them.

The bees! The bees will let themselves be lured into the most ridiculous positions. They nose their way through the thick purple brush of a thistle. They roll around in a pink peony's cup of petals. They do seem drunk on the nectar, or maybe they're just lost in their work, *busy as bees*. Some plants produce chemicals besides nectar that work on the bees like drugs, but we'll learn more about that in the next chapter.

All of this activity proves, over and over, that flowers have evolved many ways to communicate with bees, wasps, and other pollinators. They are, as I said, great communicators. But my garden also proves something else. Sometime during the millions of years of human evolution, flowers began to communicate with us. They began to work on us, to get us to help them reproduce and spread. In the process, they have come to represent so much more than a meal. They have come to represent that elusive quality—beauty.

Beauty and the Bees

Look beyond the bees and wasps and you will see that my garden is crowded with plants that have evolved to catch the human eye. These people-centered plants no longer waste time trying to attract bees, for humans have proved to be a much better partner. Some have gone so far as to stop making scent. Like the tulip, they put all their energy into producing grander and bigger and more colorful petals. Insects can't even see some of these colors, but that doesn't matter. Insects are no longer the flowers' target audience.

Those daylilies that lean forward expectantly? Wasps may still visit them, but pollination is no longer important to the plant. I'm the one who digs up their fresh tubers and plants them in new beds or gives them away so they can spread to other yards. That giant peony? It's the result of thousands of years of human intervention. Chinese poets decided the peony was the perfect representation of a woman. Therefore, Chinese gardeners and botanists selected and bred peonies that smell like perfume on human skin. It may still attract the bees, but it's designed to attract and please the human nose.

You may think that the peony is now serving humanity, that it has bent to our will. But just as we saw with the apple, the peony has entered into a partnership with people. Humans didn't invent the beauty of a peony. Since it evolved to attract insects, you could say it looked beautiful to a bee. But something about it was also beautiful to us. Then we did everything we could to make it more beautiful to our eyes (and noses).

We have spread it around the globe. I promise you, the peony isn't my servant. I spend a lot of time and energy making sure that it is happy and thriving. In return, once a year it produces colorful, richly perfumed flowers.

Forests bloom too. Pinecones give off pollen to be spread on the wind. Maples produce winged, two-part seeds that flutter to the ground. Oaks bear acorns. But it all goes on quietly (unless an acorn hits you on the head). The trees have other hidden partners, like the fungi in the soil. They don't need to put forth showy displays. But a garden in bloom or even a brightly colored wild meadow is a very different place from a forest. In a garden, you can't miss the signals. *Something is going on here.* Maybe that something special is beauty.

Flowers aren't the only organisms that use colorful displays of beauty. Many birds use this approach. Their plumes aren't just ways of getting attention. It takes a lot of energy to produce and groom their long, unusual feathers. Only a bird that is healthy and fit can pull it off. So, you could say that in nature, beauty is a sign of health. (Some birds prove their fitness by building elaborate nests, which we can assume look beautiful to their mates.)

In the same way, only a healthy plant can produce colorful blooms and the chemicals and scents needed to send a message. It's the healthiest plants that can afford the best display and sweetest nectar. Therefore, it's the healthiest plant that gets the most visits from bees or other insects. So, in a sense, the flowers are advertising their health—only they are sending the message to pollinators, not mates.

Do bees find flowers beautiful? That is a question we can never answer. But whatever is triggering the bees to be attracted to flowers also works on our human brains. That attraction may have started somewhere millions of years ago, in the need to find food. Today, it has evolved, with the flower, into something much more mysterious and powerful. It's an attraction that works on the human imagination and desire. It inspires us, and we call it beauty.

What Is Beautiful?

The beauty of flowers for humans may be hard to define. But if you want to know what a bee finds beautiful, simply look at a healthy flower. The qualities a bee finds attractive are quite specific. It begins with the petals. As I said earlier, bees don't see the same colors as we do. Green appears gray, and red to them appears as black. So, a red blossom against a green background stands out sharply. But contrasting colors aren't enough to get a bee to visit. It might simply be the contrast of a dying petal. The signal the flower sends out is much more complicated.

Some of that message is invisible to us because bees can see colors we can't, including ultraviolet light. It turns out that flowers have patterns of ultraviolet light in their petals. That means that a bee's view of a garden is very different. The petals are sending out signals that aren't meant for us. We can't really imagine them, either. It's a kind of beauty we can't experience.

There's still more information the flower holds for a bee. In addition to color, the petals send a message with their patterns. The petals are *symmetrical,* which means they consist of identical, matching parts arranged around a dividing line.

Most animals, like humans, are symmetrical. We have matching left and right sides. This is called *bilateral* symmetry, two sides that are mirror images of each other. Each side might have very minor differences, say one foot that is slightly larger than the other, but generally they match.

The sea star, or starfish, has five matching arms, arranged around a central core. This is called *radial* symmetry. Remember the core of an apple? It has five seeds arranged around a central spot. Many flowers and fruits have radial symmetry. Petals, pistils, and stamen are arranged around a central point.

Most things in nature are not symmetrical—rocks on a hillside, for example, or the placement of trees in a forest. Symmetry stands out—it's a sign that something is alive and that it has a purpose. It tells the bee that the flower is something worth investigating.

Like color, good symmetry is a sign of health in a creature. It takes a lot of extra energy to produce a neat and symmetrical flower. Disease or environmental stress can easily disturb it. Bees have evolved to seek out symmetry. You could say they find it beautiful. What's more, different types of bees prefer different types of symmetry. Honeybees favor the radial symmetry of daisies and sunflowers and clover. Bumblebees prefer the bilateral symmetry of orchids, peas, and foxgloves.

Humans too find symmetry beautiful, especially in the human face. Show someone a bunch of photos and ask them which faces are most beautiful. They will almost always pick the faces that are most symmetrical. This is true across cultures and around the world. Other physical traits might go in and out of fashion, but not that one. We also seem to be attracted to the symmetry of flowers. Perhaps that is why we sometimes speak of flowers turning their faces toward us.

Super Flowers

People everywhere find beauty in flowers. Yet there are some that stand out as special cases. These are the stars of the flower world, the blooms that poets write about, that painters paint, and that florists make money selling. These are the flowers that have, in their own way, changed history.

This doesn't mean that the daisy or the petunia or the carnation don't have their fans. But certain blooms rise above the pack. They remain in fashion and in demand for generations. The rose is one such super flower; another is the orchid, and so is the tulip.

What sets them apart? Perhaps it's their ability to change (or be changed by humans)—to have many different colors, shapes, and scents. In this way they are like the apple. Even though we use very few of its varieties, it has almost endless possibilities. There are literally hundreds of types of roses, with petals in a whole range of colors, sizes, and growing patterns. It can be pale, closed, and prim, or open, deeply colored, and heavily scented.

The same is true of orchids, one of the largest families of flowers, with thousands of species. Growing orchids is a hobby (if an expensive one) that people devote their lives to. No one spends hours collecting and breeding daisies as a hobby.

Tulips also have the ability to change to meet human desires. As we will see, the first famous tulip had a swirl of contrasting colors. Later, the big, bright, single-colored tulip became popular. Those were the type I planted as a child. As human tastes changed, the tulip changed. Whatever we wanted, the tulip was capable of becoming. The same is true for roses. That's why there are so many roses and tulips around today. By being willing partners, able to change to meet our needs, they got us to plant and reproduce them. For those flowers the path to world domination was through satisfying humanity's ever-shifting ideals of beauty.

It's difficult for us to appreciate the original beauty of the tulip, for none of them survived.

That's because like the apple, tulips don't grow true from seed. Like grafting an apple tree, the only way to make sure you have the exact same tulip flower is by cloning it. The way gardeners do this is by splitting off the small, baby bulbs that grow alongside the big one. Those small bulbs, if cared for, will grow into a new flower, a clone of the original.

However, just like apple varieties, if a type of tulip falls out of favor, and people stop planting it, it will simply disappear. But unlike trees, which can be endlessly grafted, tulip bulbs don't survive over generations. Even if tulip varieties are carefully replanted, after several generations they tend to die out. In other words, no one type of tulip can last forever. Today, one of the most popular types of tulips is a black variety called Queen of the Night.

Tulip breeders are busily seeking a new black tulip because they know the Queen of the Night is probably on her way out.

The rose and the peony, on the other hand, survive well over generations. Not only are the plants very long-lived, but they can be cloned as often as people want. That means if we want to see what a rose looked like to Shakespeare or Queen Victoria, quite likely we can find an example growing in a garden somewhere. But the only way we have of looking at historical tulips is in old paintings or book illustrations.

The Turban Flower

The rose, like the apple, has shown up in books, poems, and paintings for centuries. It's mentioned in the ancient Greek poem *The Iliad*. The tulip, on the other hand, is a latecomer. No tulip appears in the flower-crowded borders of medieval tapestries. It does not appear in early European encyclopedias that claimed to describe every type of plant in the world. It wasn't even known in Europe until 1554. That's when the Austrian ambassador to the Ottoman Empire sent home a crate of bulbs from Constantinople. (Today Constantinople is called Istanbul and it's the largest city in Turkey.) The word *tulip* comes from the Turkish word for "turban."

One reason people in Holland and other parts of Europe went mad for the tulip in the 1600s might be that to them it was still a relatively new flower. This was not the case back in Turkey, where the tulip already had many admirers. The wild tulip found there is a short, pretty, cheerful flower that looks like an open-faced, six-petaled star, often with a splotch of contrasting color at the base. They typically are red, though some are white or yellow.

Turkish gardeners had discovered that wild tulips were easily bred to have different shapes and colors. They learned to create hybrids, cross-pollinating different varieties to produce seeds. After planting the seeds, they had to wait seven years for the new flowers to appear from the bulbs. Then they could reproduce the bulbs, to get the exact same bloom in the next generation.

The Turkish botanists also discovered that tulips are prone to mutations: accidental changes in their DNA. These mutations can produce unplanned and wonderful changes in the flower's form and color. In Europe this ability to change was seen as a sign that the tulip was favored by nature. In a book about plants published in 1597, English botanist John Gerard said of the tulip that "nature seems to play more with this flower, than with any other that I do know."

The tulip's ability to change made it very adaptable. Out of all the many random variations that occurred, the ones that helped the tulip grow and reproduce survived and were passed on to the next generation. That's natural selection. Then humans came along and began to make their own selections. They helped the tulips that caught their eye, for whatever reason. It no longer mattered if those changes helped the tulip in nature by attracting insects. What mattered from then on was what attracted people.

Turkish botanists didn't learn how to breed tulips until the

1600s. But long before that, they were selecting from among the tulips growing in their gardens, helping the ones they liked the most. To Ottoman gardeners the ideal tulip was pure in color and shaped like a dagger: smooth, long, closed, and pointed. These are traits that were of no use to wild tulips, but to a domesticated tulip they were a golden ticket, ensuring human help. Those tulips have long vanished, but pictures of them survive in drawings, paintings, and on ceramic dishes and tiles.

For a time in the 1700s tulip bulbs that matched the Turkish ideal traded in Constantinople for quantities of gold. This was during the reign of Sultan Ahmed III, from 1703 to 1730, a period known to Turkish historians as the *Lale Devri,* or Tulip Era. The sultan was ruled by his passion for the flower, so much so that he imported bulbs by the millions from Holland, where the Dutch had become masters of large-scale bulb production.

Each spring for a period of weeks the imperial gardens were filled with prize tulips. Each variety was marked with a label made from silver. Tulips whose petals had opened too wide were held shut with fine threads.

In addition to tulips growing in soil, there were thousands of cut stems held in glass bottles. Their numbers were multiplied by mirrors placed around the garden. Songbirds in gilded cages supplied music, and hundreds of giant tortoises carrying candles on their backs lumbered through the gardens, providing light. All the guests were required to dress in colors that matched the tulips. The whole scene was repeated every night for as long as the tulips were in bloom. The yearly festival cost a fortune and the expense in the end proved the sultan's downfall. His waste of the national treasure on tulips led to a revolt and his overthrow.

Stolen Beauty

Today most people think of Holland as the home of tulips. But as we've seen, the flower had to be brought to that country. What's more, the history of tulips in Holland begins with a theft. A French botanist named Carolus Clusius was the victim.

Clusius was perhaps the most important European botanist of his time. Bulbs were his specialty, and he's credited with the introduction of many flowering bulbs to Europe, including irises, hyacinths, anemones, daffodils, lilies, and of course tulips. He was in a good position to get the bulbs because he was director of the Austrian Empire's Imperial Botanical Garden in Vienna.

In 1593, Clusius moved to Leiden in Holland and he took some tulip bulbs with him. These were not the first tulips in Holland, but the ones Clusius brought were different and rare. Not only that, he made a big deal of keeping his rare tulips to himself. He wouldn't sell or share any seeds. This enraged Dutch gardeners and they broke into his garden at night and stole his best flowers, bulbs and all. A discouraged Clusius gave up growing tulips, but the thieves quickly bred the stolen blooms and distributed the seeds until the "rare" new tulips were found across Holland.

Note that the stolen tulips were reproduced by seed, not bulbs. As I mentioned earlier, tulips, like apples, do not come true from seed—their offspring bear little resemblance to their parents. This means that what the tulip thieves spread across Holland was a wild array of differently shaped and colored tulips. This original sowing by seed may well be the source of much of the astounding variety of Dutch tulips.

The modern tulip has become such a cheap and common commodity that it's hard for us to understand the glamour that once surrounded the flower. The Dutch were so proud of their botanical treasure that they listed it in the same breath as their mighty navy and their democratic government. The excitement the flower produced might have had something to do with its roots in Asia, at that time a place of intrigue because few had visited there. The tulip offered beauty and color in a land where everyone, regardless of social class, dressed remarkably alike, in blacks, browns, and grays. The color of tulips was like no color anyone had ever laid eyes on before: rich, brilliant, and more intense than that of any other flower. To the Dutch eye, it was beautiful. Rare and sought-after varieties began to sell for high prices in Holland and other European countries.

In France in 1608, a miller exchanged his entire mill for a single bulb of a variety called "Mère Brune" or "brown mother." Around the same time a bridegroom accepted a single tulip as the whole of his wife's dowry. He did so happily, it was reported, and the variety became known as "Mariage de ma fille" or "my daughter's wedding." (A dowry was a custom among middle class or wealthy people. It was the amount of wealth a bride was supposed to contribute to a marriage.)

Yet despite these examples, tulipomania never reached the pitch in France and England that it would in Holland. Why did the craze take hold among the Dutch, who liked to think of themselves as a serious and clearheaded people?

Perhaps it was because the Dutch were already in the habit of changing and controlling nature. After all, most of the country should, by all rights, be under water. Its other name, the Netherlands, means "low-lying country." Only a complex system of canals and dikes (or dams) keeps the ocean back and the land drained. The windmill, which exists in many places around the world, became a symbol of the Dutch ability to harness nature.

Land in Holland was scarce and expensive, and Dutch gardens were miniatures, measured in square feet rather than acres. Like the Ottoman sultan, the Dutch sometimes used mirrors to make their plots seem bigger. With space so limited, Dutch gardeners tried to make a statement with every flower they planted. They sought out original and unusual blooms and in the 1600s the tall, boldly colored tulip fit their needs exactly.

Botany became a national pastime for the Dutch, followed as closely and eagerly as we follow sports today. A book about plants could become a best seller. A botanist like Clusius was a celebrity. In the seventeenth century, the Dutch were the richest people in Europe and they liked to show off their riches. Flower gardens, which do not produce food or make money, have always been a way for the wealthy to display their wealth. In fact, the more useless a flower, meaning the more it is only a display of beauty and nothing else, the more it becomes a show of how wealthy the gardener is.

A Useful Tulip

In Europe until the 1500s, most of the flowers grown on farms or in gardens were sources of medicine, perfume, or even food. They may have been beautiful, but they were also useful. The Puritans and other Protestant groups only believed in growing things if they had a practical purpose. Growing a flower for its beauty was seen as a form of pride or vanity. The Pilgrims and other Puritans who came to the Americas would never have brought a flower that did not have some medicinal or other benefit.

When the tulip first arrived in Europe, people set about finding some practical use for it. The Germans boiled and sugared the bulbs and declared them a delicacy. The English tried serving them up with oil and vinegar. Herbalists said the tulip could keep you from passing gas. However, none of these uses caught on. Try as people might, the tulip remained really good at just one thing—producing beauty.

As a new arrival, the tulip was free from any association with religion or European culture of the past. Unlike the apple or the rose, the tulip had not yet been enlisted as a symbol of religion. There were no legends or poems written about it. It was a blank canvas that the Dutch could interpret as they liked. It is also a simple, easy-to-understand plant with one flower on every stem, one stem on every plant. Tulips usually have no scent and its petals curve inward. You could almost say that for a flower it is modest.

Yet none of those qualities are enough to explain the total insanity the tulip produced in Holland. There is one more reason to consider: To the Dutch, the tulip was a magic flower because every now and then a single bloom would appear that carried a strange pattern of colors. It would happen in perhaps one out of every hundred tulips that were planted. A yellow or white flower would open to reveal petals covered with fine, swirling lines of vivid contrasting color.

Tulips with these feathery or flame-like patterns were said to have been "broken." A broken tulip with the right kind of pattern was worth a fortune. If the flames of the contrasting color reached to the petal's lip or if the pattern was symmetrical, the owner of that bulb had won the lottery.

You'll remember that American orchard owners who found a tasty variety of apple growing on their farm could graft it and produce trees that bore the same exact fruit. Dutch gardeners who found a broken tulip magically appearing in their fields could split off the small offsets from its bulb. Those baby bulbs would grow into tulips with the exact same colors and patterns. Bulbs for broken tulips commanded a fantastic price. The price was driven even higher because for some unknown reason the bulbs of broken tulips produced fewer and smaller offsets, making them even rarer.

Broken Beauty

The most famous such break was a bloom called the Semper Augustus. It was a white tulip with feathery swirls of bright carmine red sitting in a blue base. This wild bloom was the opposite of the simple, solid-colored, orderly tulips that dotted the Dutch countryside. It was new, exciting, and striking with almost uncontrolled patterns of color.

People believed that Semper Augustus was the most beautiful flower in the world, a masterpiece. In the 1620s there were only a dozen or so specimens in existence and most of them were owned by Dr. Adriaen Pauw. Pauw was a merchant, a director of the new East India Company, one of the world's first corporations, set up to import textiles and spices from India. Pauw was also a passionate tulip collector. He grew them on his estate near the town of Haarlem, where, like others, he used mirrors in his garden to multiply the effect of his precious blooms.

Through the 1620s, Dr. Pauw was bombarded with offers to buy his Semper Augustus bulbs, but he would not part with them at any price. His refusal may only have driven buyers' interest to greater heights. But Pauw judged the pleasure of looking at a Semper Augustus far greater than any profit.

Dutch growers, seeking to copy the popularity of Semper Augustus, would resort to all sorts of measures to make their tulips break. For example, they would sprinkle powdered paint on a bed planted with white tulips, on the theory that rainwater would wash the color down into the soil, where it would be taken up by the bulb.

They invented all sorts of recipes guaranteed to produce the magic color breaks. Some contained pigeon droppings or plaster dust taken from the walls of old houses. Now and then the treatments would be followed with a good break. This was just random chance, but it made it seem as though their efforts were working. The attempts to break tulips continued.

What the Dutch could not have known was that the patterns of broken tulips were caused by a virus. The color of any tulip consists of two pigments working together. There is always a base color of yellow or white. There's also a second color, called an anthocyanin. The solid color we see in the petals is a mix of the base color and the second color. The virus holds back and changes the production of the anthocyanin so it appears in fine, curling lines.

It wasn't until the 1920s, after the invention of the electron microscope, that scientists discovered the disease, called the mosaic virus. It was spread from tulip to tulip by a tiny insect, the peach potato aphid. The virus not only changed the color of the tulips but made them weaker, which is why the offsets of broken tulips were so small and few in number.

By that time, producing tulip bulbs was a giant industry in Holland. The growers didn't want any diseases weakening their crops. Just as apple growers at that time were standardizing their industry, selecting only a few varieties to grow and sell, the tulip growers of Holland wanted their industry to go smoothly with no pesky infections. They sought to rid their fields of the virus. Color breaks, when they did occur, were promptly destroyed.

The story of the virus and the tulip is a strange one. A disease made the tulip weaker and less able to reproduce. That would normally be an evolutionary dead end. But at the same time, the virus made the flower seem more beautiful to people. It changed a simple, tame bloom into something wild and unpredictable. Broken tulips were highly sought after precisely because they were so different and untamed. For a few hundred years, the sickest tulips were the best at attracting human partners.

To fully understand what happened, we must consider one other player—the virus itself. By accidentally producing a flower that humans considered more beautiful, the virus was able to get people to help it spread. The more beautiful the breaks produced by the infection, the greater the number of infected plants in Dutch gardens and the more total virus in circulation. What a trick! Where beauty had once signaled health, it now signaled illness—only the tulip planters of Holland didn't know that. As soon as they did, they set out to get rid of the sickly plants.

The closest we have to a broken tulip today is the group known as the Rembrandts. They are named that because they resemble the broken tulips painted by the famous Dutch artist Rembrandt. But these modern-day tulips are not the result of an infection by a virus. They have been bred to have two-color patterns, and they can be reliably reproduced, and mass marketed. Compare them to the paintings of the broken tulips of Rembrandt's time and they don't really hold their own. The patterns of the modern flowers look heavy and clumsy, as if painted in haste with a thick brush. The petals of broken tulips could seem both bold and delicate at once. In the most striking examples—such as the Semper Augustus—the outbreak of color could be breathtaking.

Tulipomania

Dr. Adriaen Pauw could have named his price for a single bulb of Semper Augustus. As I've noted, it was very rare, and very unusual. Although he wouldn't sell, other broken tulips fetched huge sums. Slowly, the market for unusual tulips grew. After all, if a single Semper Augustus bulb was worth a large mansion, who was to say that a different variety wasn't worth as much, or more? Growers began to wonder how much they could get for their own special tulips. Maybe they too were sitting on a gold mine.

That kind of thinking drove tulip prices higher and higher. By the 1630s the market for tulips was taken over by *speculation*. People were no longer buying tulips in order to plant them and enjoy them or show them off. They bought bulbs solely in the hope of turning around and selling them at a profit. The tulip was no longer a source of beauty, it became a source of wealth.

This kind of market is sometimes called a bubble, because prices rise like a bubble, but also because sooner or later, like a bubble, the market bursts. In a bubble, people believe that prices for something will continue to rise no matter what. That belief helps make prices rise, at least for a while. For if you're sure that prices for tulip bulbs will be higher tomorrow, you will be willing to pay more for them today. As long as you're convinced that tulip prices will keep going up, then the sky's the limit. As long as you can find someone else who also believes it, someone who will buy your bulbs at a higher price, the bubble keeps rising.

By 1635, the tulip bubble in Holland was rising like crazy. It seemed that everyone, the rich and the poor, was trying to cash in, buying and selling tulips in the hope of making a fortune. But the autumn of 1635 marked a turning point. That's when people stopped buying and selling real bulbs. Instead, they began trading in the promise of bulbs. The notes listed the details of the flowers, their colors, the dates they would be delivered, and their price.

Before then, the tulip market followed the rhythm of the season. Bulbs could change hands only between the months of June, when they were lifted from the ground, and October, when they had to be planted again. Wild as it was, the market before 1635 was still rooted in reality: cash money for actual flowers. Now began what the Dutch called the *windhandel*—the wind trade.

Suddenly the tulip trade was a year-round affair. Joining in were legions of speculators who knew nothing about tulips. They were carpenters and weavers, woodcutters and glass blowers, smiths, cobblers, coffee grinders, tradesmen, peddlers, clergymen, teachers, and lawyers. One burglar in Amsterdam pawned the tools of his trade so that he too could become a speculator in tulips.

Rushing to get in on the sure thing, these people sold their businesses, mortgaged their homes, and invested their life savings in slips of paper representing future flowers. This flood of new money drove prices to extreme heights. In the space of a month the price of a red-and-yellow-striped bulb called *Gheel ende Root van Leyden* leaped from 46 guilders to 515. A bulb of *Switsers,* a yellow tulip feathered with red, soared from 60 to 1,800 guilders.

At its height, the trade in tulips was conducted by florists trading in "colleges." These were back rooms of taverns given over to the new business. Colleges quickly developed a set of rituals that sound like a cross between orderly stock market rules and a drinking contest.

Under one common set of procedures, a buyer and seller who wanted to do business were handed slates on which they each wrote an opening price for the tulip in question. The slates were then passed to a pair of neutral traders who settled on a price somewhere between the two opening bids. They wrote this compromise on the slates and handed them back to the buyer and seller, who could let the number stand or rub it out.

If both rubbed out the price, the deal was off. But if only one trader declined, that florist had to pay a fine to the college. When a deal did close, the buyer had to pay a small fee to the college. That was called the *wijnkoopsgeld:* wine money. In fact, all the fines and commissions were used to buy wine and beer for everyone.

The Greater Fool

The logic of a bubble market has been given a name: "the greater fool theory." Although we may think only a fool would pay a fortune for a single tulip bulb, it makes sense as long as there is an even greater fool out there willing to pay still more. By 1636 the taverns were crowded with such people, and as long as there were always more people joining in, ready to spend their life's fortunes, the bubble continued to rise.

But every bubble sooner or later must burst. In Holland that event came in the winter of 1637. On February 2 of that year, the florists of Haarlem gathered as usual to auction bulbs in one of the tavern colleges. A florist sought to begin the bidding at 1,250 guilders for a quantity of tulips. Finding no takers, he tried again at 1,100, then 1,000. All at once everyone in the room understood that the market had changed. Where days before they would have paid those sums, now no one was willing to do so. There were no more greater fools.

Haarlem was the capital of the bulb trade, and the news that there were no buyers to be found there shot across the country. Within days tulip bulbs were unsellable at any price. People were ruined, especially the common working people who had sold everything they owned to buy tulip bulbs that were now worthless.

Afterward, in trying to explain the tulipomania, many Dutch blamed the flower for their folly, as if the tulips themselves had lured otherwise sensible people to their ruin. Some even took their anger out on the flower. In the months after the fever broke, a professor of botany at the University of Leiden could be seen walking the streets of the city, beating any tulip he encountered with his cane.

Today, the Dutch tulip craze is held up as an example of market speculation, a warning against market bubbles. Sadly, it's a warning that usually goes ignored. In just the last few decades we've seen market bubbles in the United States for high-tech stocks, real estate, and even Beanie Babies.

It is sometimes lost that though tulipomania destroyed the savings of many Dutch, it also laid the foundation for the Dutch bulb business. Today, growing and selling tulips is a modern, mechanized industry worth almost eight billion dollars a year.

As we've seen, this industry has transformed the tulip into a uniform commodity, banishing the strange oddities caused by the mosaic virus. The modern tulip is meant to be seen in groups, massed in garden borders and hillsides. These tulips appear to us as instances of pure color; they could almost be lollipops or lipsticks in the landscape. In part because they are so cheap and plentiful, we can easily forget to look at them individually. Because they are so uniform, you might not even bother. After all, you might think, every tulip looks pretty much like every other tulip, doesn't it?

Queen of the Night

One spring I decided to slow down and try to look at just one tulip at a time, to see if I could recover a sense of the beauty of the flower. I had the feeling that if cut and brought indoors and then really looked at, a single flower would hold the power to astonish. And that is what I found. When you look at just one tulip closely, you understand why painters, illustrators, and photographers so often choose the tulip as their subject. I think this is true even if you look at an individual of the everyday varieties, like the Triumphs and Darwin bulbs sold in the mass-market mesh bags. But I chose one that was a little different, the almost black variety called Queen of the Night.

Queen of the Night is as close to black as a flower gets, though in fact it is a very dark and glossy purple. It is so dark that it appears to absorb more light than it reflects, a kind of floral black hole. This effect, a black or nearly black tulip, was prized by the Dutch, and the quest for a truly black tulip became one of the stranger subplots of tulipomania. Alexandre Dumas, author of *The Three Musketeers,* wrote a whole novel—*The Black Tulip*—about a competition in seventeenth-century Holland to grow the first truly black tulip. The plot revolves around a prize offered of 100,000 guilders and the greed inspired by the contest that winds up destroying three lives.

What is the lure of a *black* tulip? Perhaps because the color black is so rare in the plant world. The broken tulips such as Semper Augustus were sought after in part because they were so rare. Perhaps a black tulip seems to be the opposite of the bright reds, yellows, and oranges that are so common.

Looking at my own black tulip here on my desk, I try to appreciate it as an individual. The first thing I notice is the classic form of the single tulip. It has six petals arrayed in two layers: three inner petals cupped inside three outer ones. The six petals together form a vault of space around the stamens and pistil. They shelter them from view but at the same time, advertise what is inside.

I see too that the petals are not identical. The inner petals are notched and the outer petals have smooth uninterrupted edges as clean as a blade's. All the petals look soft and silky but are not: To the touch they're unexpectedly hard. They form a tailored, somewhat simple blossom. The fact that Queen of the Night has no noticeable scent proves this is an experience designed strictly for the eye.

The long, curving stem of my Queen of the Night is nearly as beautiful as the flower it supports. It is graceful but strong, like the curving steel cables of a suspension bridge. The curve seems perfectly designed to hold the bloom, and of course it has evolved to do just that.

As the day warms, the curve of the stem relaxes and the petals pull back to reveal the pistils and stamen, inviting any insect that wants to pollinate it. Six stamens—one for every petal—circle around a sturdy upright pedestal, each holding a powdery yellow bouquet of pollen. The crown of the central green pistil is called the stigma. It has a pursed set of slightly crooked lips (typically three) poised to receive the grains of pollen. From there they will be conducted downward toward the flower's ovary. Sometimes a single glistening droplet of liquid nectar appears on the stigma's lip.

To me, everything about the tulip seems neat, clear, and orderly, in contrast to the wilder, louder rose or peony. Those show-offs have double and triple blooms, ruffled edges, and ridiculous numbers of petals. One Chinese tree peony is said to have more than three hundred. For them, one flower per stem isn't enough—they have multiple blooms on each plant or vine. On top of that, they have fragrances that can overwhelm our senses. Lean in and inhale the scent of a rose or peony and you're likely to forget yourself for a moment.

It's true that there are a few tulip varieties like the parrot that attempt a beauty that is a little more complicated. They have ruffled edge petals or two-tone flowers. But those are breeders' inventions created as alternatives to the true tulip. The classic tulip has a clean, steely stem that holds a single, clean-lined flower up in the air for our admiration. Even when they die, they do so gracefully. Instead of turning to mush, like a spent rose, the six petals on a tulip cleanly, dryly open, and then drop, often at the same time.

Yet even the orderly tulip isn't untouched by the random-ness of nature. If I walk out into my garden when the tulips are in bloom, I will sometimes find flowers with nine and even ten petals. There might be mutant stigmas with six lips instead of three. Once I found a Queen of the Night with a leaf streaked with deep purple. It looked as though somehow the purple of the flower had seeped down into the dull green leaves.

As gardeners have known for generations, tulips are prone to such random changes. There are chance mutations, color breaks, and cases of what growers call "thievery." Thievery is said to happen when certain flowers in a field revert to the form and color of their parent.

The Birth of Beauty

I recently passed by the square in front of the Plaza Hotel in Manhattan where a large flower bed had been planted with thou-sands of fat yellow Triumphs. They were laid out in a precise, almost military grid and they were exactly the sort of stiff, primary-colored tulips I used to plant in my parents' yard.

I'd read that even today, at a time when tulip growers struggle to keep their fields free of the virus that causes the flower to break, it still occasionally happens. And there in the middle of that monotonous flower bed, I spotted one—a broken tulip. It was a violent eruption of red on what should have been a pure canary yellow. It wasn't the most handsome of breaks, but the flare of red on that one bloom stood out like a mischievous clown. It completely wrecked the controlled order the flower bed was meant to represent.

There was something thrilling about it—I could hardly believe my luck. To me that careless splash of red seemed almost like a trip through time to the distant tulip past. The virus had managed to live on and do its work, creating new, strange patterns. I felt I was witnessing a great, underground force of nature that could not be held back, no matter how people tried to control it.

Once upon a time, two hundred million years ago, there were no flowers. There were plants, including ferns, mosses, and conifers, but these plants don't form true flowers or fruit. (Conifers are evergreens, usually trees that produce *cones,* which is how they get their name.) Some of those plants reproduced asexually, cloning themselves by various means. The plants that did reproduce sexually, like conifers, did so by releasing pollen onto the wind or water. Only by chance would that tiny grain find its way to other members of the species, and a tiny, primitive seed would result.

This pre-flower world was a simpler, sleepier world than our own. Plant evolution proceeded more slowly, there being so much less mixing of genes than sexual reproduction allows. It was a plainer-looking world, greener even than it is now, but without all the colors and patterns (not to mention scents) that flowers and fruits would bring into it.

Flowers changed everything. Botanists call the plants that form flowers "angiosperms." They appeared during the Cretaceous period, about 140 million years ago, and spread over the earth with stunning rapidity. (Rapid in evolutionary terms.) They spread so rapidly because they had help. Instead of relying on wind or water to move their seeds around, a flowering plant that produced fruit or seeds could enlist the help of an animal by offering food for transportation.

Meanwhile bees and other pollinators helped genes to mix by carrying pollen from plant to plant. This allowed flowering plants to produce more varied offspring. As we saw with the apple, producing many new varieties means at least some of your offspring will be better suited to new and changing habitats.

The flower introduced a whole new level of collaboration among species. They did this by evolving ways to attract partners. Food like nectar and fruit were the offerings that flowering plants made to animals, including people. But the plants had to advertise their offerings to attract their partners. Another name for that attraction is beauty. Beauty to a bee or a hummingbird looks different than to a human. They may even see colors that we cannot. But it's still beauty—something they want to go to and experience.

To gain partners, flowering plants had to give up independence. They could no longer reproduce without help. Their ability to attract partners, their ability to produce beauty, became the key to their survival. Plants that produced flowers that were better at attracting partners, that were more beautiful to pollinators, were rewarded.

So was specialization. After all, it doesn't help a rose if an insect delivers its pollen to a tulip or vice versa. Flowers that attracted just one specialized pollinator could ensure their pollen would wind up in the right flower—one of their own species. The advantage of having one dedicated partner, rather than several, drove plants to develop distinct blooms that looked different from any other. This is the main reason we can enjoy flowers in so many shapes and colors. The other reason, of course, is the work of human gardeners. But evolution created the variety; we humans only expanded it.

Over time, humans entered into the natural history of the flower. Like other animals, we were attracted by the food flowers produced, as with the apple. But we also learned to recognize the beauty that advertised the food. Flowers that were more beautiful to us were more successful in gaining our attention. At some point, the seeds and the fruit became unnecessary—the beauty alone was all the plant needed to get our help. No one plants tulips for food. We plant them for their beauty.

The plants produced flowers we found beautiful, and we, their partners, did our share, multiplying them far beyond anything they could have accomplished on their own. We moved their seeds (or bulbs) around the planet, writing poems, inventing fairy tales, and painting pictures to spread their fame and ensure their success.

And what about us? How did we make out? We did very well by the flower. How could you possibly measure the pleasure that billions of humans have had looking at a single bud in a backyard or walking through an elegant garden? Once again, we can see we've formed a partnership with plants, and once more we have gotten our reward, only this time it's not food or sweetness, but something harder to measure—beauty.

Chapter Three

Desire: *Energy*

Plant: *Coffee and Tea*

I will start this chapter with a confession. Halfway through writing it, I almost quit.

I'd been chugging merrily along, conducting interviews, reading, traveling to South America to visit a coffee farm, and tasting dozens of varieties of coffee and tea. I was excited, interested, convinced (as usual) that I was on the trail of a great story. Then suddenly, I lost all confidence. I began to ask myself, was it all worth the effort? Would anyone even want to read my words? Why had I ever started it?

What had happened to cause this sudden crisis? The answer was right in front of me, or rather, it was no longer in front of me. I'd decided that to write a piece about coffee and tea it would be a good idea to stop drinking both of them. So, I just quit. I gave up my regular tall morning cup of joe, my several glasses of green tea through the day, and my occasional cappuccino after lunch.

And of course, by giving up coffee and tea, I also gave up caffeine. I went cold turkey on a drug I'd been happily using for years. My sudden lack of confidence was the result of caffeine withdrawal.

Did I really say it was a *good* idea?

The Caffeine Partnership

We've seen how plants have offered people sweetness (apples and other fruits). They've offered us beauty (tulips and other flowers). These offerings have resulted in successful partnerships

101

between plants and humans. We take the gifts the plants offer and in return we help them spread and reproduce.

In this chapter, I want to examine another very different sort of partnership between plants and people. It's a partnership based on a chemical: a drug called 1,3,7-trimethylxanthine, a tiny organic molecule known to most of us as caffeine.

Caffeine is made by dozens of plants, but the two you're most familiar with are coffee and tea. Their scientific names are *Coffea* and *Camellia sinensis*. These plants evolved to produce caffeine because it works on insect brains. For example, it changes the behavior of bees in ways that help the plant. (We'll talk more about this a little later in the chapter.)

It turns out that chemicals that work on insect brains can also work on human brains. Caffeine changes our behavior, and our moods, how we think and how we act. It's also very habit-forming. Once we humans discovered caffeine, we began working to get more of it. We formed a partnership with coffee and tea and spread them far beyond their original homes. We made them two of the world's most successful plants, right up there with the edible grasses—rice, wheat, and corn.

But unlike those plants, which offer humans food, coffee and tea offer the ability to change our mood. Unlike rice, wheat, or corn, we don't eat tea or coffee. We pick their beans (coffee) or leaves (tea) and then ship those beans or leaves all over the globe. When they arrive in our homes or coffee shops, we grind up the beans or the leaves, soak them in hot water, and extract the caffeine and some flavor. Then we dump the remains—that is, almost all of the plant—in the garbage or compost. We don't really want the plant. We just want the caffeine.

Kids and Caffeine

We don't always think of caffeine as a drug, but that's what it is. It's the most widely used drug on the planet. Perhaps 90 percent of all adult humans use it on a regular basis. It's also the only drug we let children buy. More than 70 percent of kids in the United States use caffeine daily, mostly in soft drinks and so-called energy drinks.

The American Academy of Pediatrics says children under twelve should not use caffeine at all. (Pediatrics is the branch of medicine that deals with the care of children.) They also recommend no more than 100 milligrams of caffeine for people ages twelve to eighteen. How much is that? One eight-ounce cup of coffee has about 150 milligrams of caffeine. One sixteen-ounce can of energy drink might have as much as 300 milligrams.

Kids should be careful about using caffeine for many reasons. Caffeine is powerful. Using caffeine during the day can make it hard to sleep at night. It might give you a shot of energy, but that wears off and leaves you feeling more tired than before. Other symptoms of caffeine withdrawal are headaches, an inability to concentrate, lack of confidence, and a depressed mood. Also, your body gets used to caffeine, so the more you use it, the more you need to feel its effects.

As you'll see from my own experience, many adults don't realize how dependent we are on our daily dose of caffeine. That's why, for adults or kids alike, if you're going to use caffeine, you should know what you're getting into. Caffeine has some impressive benefits, as we will see, but like any drug, it has downsides as well.

Caffeine is only one of many psychoactive or brain-affecting drugs we get from plants. Throughout human history, people have used plants to ease pain or change their moods. Traditional medicine in many cultures depends on the ability of some plants to affect human biology. For example, an early form of aspirin was made from willow bark. Digitalis, an early heart medication, was made from plants like the foxglove.

Today, scientists continue to make medicine from plants, including drugs that fight cancer and other diseases. And of course, many illegal and dangerous drugs like opium and cocaine are made from plants. Many of these plants have formed their own partnerships with humans, but in this chapter, we're going to focus on coffee and tea.

Quitting Caffeine

Like the great majority of caffeine users, I didn't give it much thought. My morning coffee and afternoon tea were just a part of my routine. Which also meant, whatever caffeine was doing to my brain seemed like my normal state of mind. After years of drinking coffee and tea, I no longer knew what my brain was like when it *wasn't* on caffeine.

I decided I'd better find out. I just never realized that giving up caffeine would make it harder for me to *write about* caffeine. Looking back, I should have expected it. I knew about all the caffeine withdrawal symptoms. I just didn't realize how extremely difficult writing would be when I couldn't concentrate and had lost all confidence.

The first day of my withdrawal was by far the most trying. I had postponed the day as long as I could, making up the kinds of excuses every addict does. "I have a stressful week coming up," I would tell myself. "Not a good time to quit." This went on for weeks. Eventually, I found I'd done all the other work I needed. Quitting caffeine to see what it was like was the only bit of research left to do. I settled on April tenth and stuck to it.

That morning, I found that without my usual cup of coffee, the prospect of writing, or even just reading, seemed impossible. I was caught in the feelings of caffeine withdrawal. In fact, my withdrawal had actually begun the night before while I was sleeping. That's when coffee drinkers are at their low point. The caffeine we took in the day before has worn off. But we sleep through this low point. Then we wake up and have some more. The day's first cup feels powerful because it stops the unpleasant withdrawal feelings that are just starting to build up.

This is one of the hidden powers of caffeine. It works perfectly with the natural rhythms of our bodies. Our morning cup of coffee arrives just in time to head off the looming misery set in motion by yesterday's cup of coffee. Every day, caffeine solves the problem caffeine creates. What a neat trick.

My usual morning ritual, after breakfast and exercise at home, involves a half-mile walk with my wife, Judith, to our local coffee shop, a place called the Cheese Board. This day, I was conducting an experiment, using myself as a guinea pig. I made sure to keep everything about the morning ritual unchanged, except that when I reached the front of the line, I forced myself to ask for a mint tea. After years of "the usual," the barista raised an eyebrow.

I carried my mint tea in the same type of cardboard cup and sat and sipped it in the same place, just as I would my coffee. Of course, without caffeine, it didn't do what I wanted. The mental fog I'd woken up with never vanished. The clarity and focus that coffee brings never arrived. I didn't feel terrible—I never got a headache, but I never felt fully awake. At home, I tried writing, but without much success. "I feel like an unsharpened pencil," I wrote in my notebook.

By noon I really missed what my wife calls her "cup of optimism." That is one effect of caffeine—it lifts your mood. But what I really missed was my normal ability to think clearly. I began to worry that my ability to think and write came only from consuming caffeine. Was I helpless without it?

Over the course of the next few days, I began to feel better. I realized much of the fogginess I had experienced was a symptom of caffeine withdrawal. I could think clearly, yet I still didn't feel quite right. The world seemed a duller, less interesting place. Mornings were the worst. Waking up took a lot longer and I never felt fully awake, not the way I had before quitting.

I could function without caffeine, but I missed it. Like much of the human race, I'd come to completely rely on it. Without the help of coffee or tea, I just didn't feel like myself.

Insect Control

This is an astonishing accomplishment for a plant. Others may have captured our taste buds or our gaze or sense of smell, but coffee and tea have captured our very minds. They captured our minds so completely that we worked to wildly expand their numbers and habitats.

Coffee originally grew in a few corners of East Africa and Southern Arabia. It now circles the globe. We humans have cut down and rooted out other plants to give coffee more than twenty-seven million acres in which to grow. Tea, or *Camellia sinensis*, has spread from its origins in Southwest China (near present-day Myanmar and Tibet) as far west as India and Africa and east to Japan. We have set aside ten million acres for it.

Of course, coffee and tea plants didn't plan this. Over millions of years of evolution, through blind chance, they each began to produce the caffeine molecule. So did other plants. For example, chocolate, which is made from the beans of the cacao plant, also contains caffeine.

Once they began to produce it, caffeine helped the plants in several ways. First, it's a defense against predators. At high doses, it is lethal to insects. Its bitter flavor may also discourage pests from eating plants that produce it. This may be why the leaves of the coffee shrub contain more caffeine than its beans. Caffeine also appears to have herbicidal properties. That means it can stop other plants from growing. This removes competition for soil, sunlight, and water.

For all these reasons, plants that produced caffeine had an advantage over other plants. They could discourage pests and capture more territory. Scientists would say caffeine gave those plants an evolutionary advantage. Yet there is more to this story.

Caffeine may be lethal to insects at high doses, but at lower doses it does something quite interesting. It changes insect behavior. For example, it reduces their appetite. (It does this in humans too.) That is very useful if you want to stop an insect from eating your leaves.

Caffeine also seems to mix up the insect mind. In a famous experiment conducted by NASA in the 1990s, researchers fed a variety of drugs to spiders to see how they would affect their web-making skills. Spiders on caffeine lost the ability to weave useful webs. The threads had no definite pattern, met at weird angles, and had openings big enough to let small birds through.

In evolutionary terms, changing your enemy's behavior may be a better strategy than killing it. Poison may work on most of your pests, but there will always be individual insects that are more resistant to the poison than others. Some of those resistant insects will survive and have offspring and soon you have a whole new breed of insect that can happily eat the poisoned leaves. It might be a better strategy to just ruin your enemy's appetite or distract it—in other words, change its behavior. The insect won't do as much damage and its offspring will still be affected by your drug.

Caffeinated Bees

So far, there is nothing in the story of caffeine that explains its great appeal to humans. But it turns out that some plants make caffeine not to repel insects, but to attract them.

In the 1990s, German researchers made the surprising discovery that several types of plants, including coffee and tea, produce caffeine in their nectar. Nectar, as we have seen in previous chapters, is the sugar-filled liquid that plants produce to attract bees and other pollinators. How could it help plants to add the bitter and possibly poisonous caffeine to the sweet nectar in its flowers? Wouldn't that repel pollinators rather than attract them?

The scientists were puzzled. Perhaps this was just an accident. Perhaps the caffeine was leaking into the nectar from other parts of the plant. Or could it serve some other purpose?

In 2013, a young scientist named Geraldine Wright decided to perform a simple experiment. I spoke to her about her work. She told me she built a sort of honeybee apartment grid. Each bee was held in its own little compartment with only their heads poking out on top. Using a medicine dropper, Wright fed her bees various mixtures of sugar water and caffeine.

Each time she offered a bee a drop of mixture, she gave them a little puff of a strong scent. The idea, she said, was to see how quickly they learned to associate that scent with a food source. Each mixture had its own scent.

"Really simple, low tech, no funding," she told me, describing the setup. Okay, but how do you know when a bee likes something? "That's simple too," Wright explained. "They extend their mouth parts if they want something." Basically, they stick their tongues out. The idea was when the bees smelled a scent, and wanted that mixture, they would stick out their tongues.

Wright discovered that her bees were more likely to remember and prefer scents that went with caffeine mixtures. They remembered those smells better than scents that went with "nectar" of only sugar. Even if the mixture contained tiny amounts of caffeine, too little for the bees to taste, they remembered and preferred those mixtures to the ones with only sugar.

Now we can understand how adding caffeine to nectar helps a plant. It causes a pollinator to remember that flower and return to it more often. Drug your pollinator with a low dose of caffeine and she will remember you and come back for more. She will choose you over other plants that don't offer the same drug.

We don't know how bees feel when they drink caffeinated nectar. All we know is that the caffeine helps them remember. Further experiments have proven Wright's discovery. Bees will remember and return more reliably to flowers that offer them caffeinated nectar.

One experiment found that bees were four times more likely to return to the caffeinated flowers than to flowers offering nectar only. The power of the caffeine is so great that bees will keep returning to a flower even when there is no nectar left.

This really isn't good for the bees. They need nectar to produce honey for their winter stores. Going back to flowers with no nectar is a waste of their time and energy. Caffeine in the nectar means the partnership between plant and animal is no longer equal. The plant more or less drugs the bees, forcing them to act in ways that are against their interests. The caffeine has triggered something in their brains that makes them keep going back.

When I learned that, it sounded strangely familiar.

We Discover Caffeine

Could we humans be in the same boat as those bees? Have we too been drugged by caffeinated plants to act against our interest in the process? With apples and tulips, we could see the benefits to both sides of the partnership. Is our partnership with tea and coffee just as equal?

One way to answer this is to look at the history of coffee and humans. That might allow us to judge how caffeine-producing plants have changed our behavior.

We can start with tea since humans started using that first. It has been used as a medicine in China since at least 1000 BC. One of the earliest uses of tea was by Buddhist monks, who sipped tea to stay awake during long meditation sessions. By AD 900 tea had become a popular beverage in China.

Coffee is believed to have been discovered in Ethiopia around AD 850. That is one of a handful of places where the shrubby tree grows wild. The story goes that a goatherd named Kaldi noticed how his herd would behave strangely and remain awake all night after eating the red berries of the *Coffea* plant. Kaldi told this to the abbot of a local monastery. The monk made a drink with the berries and so became the first person to get a coffee buzz. At least, that's the legend.

What we know for certain is that by the 1400s, coffee was being grown in East Africa and traded across the Arabian Peninsula. At first, the new drink was used mainly as an aid to concentration. Like the Buddhists of China, Sufi Muslims in Yemen used caffeine to keep them from dozing off during long religious practices.

Within a century, coffeehouses had sprung up in cities across the Arab world. In 1570 there were more than six hundred of them in Constantinople alone. The shops spread north and west through the Ottoman Empire, which ruled the Middle East, North Africa, and parts of Eastern Europe.

These coffeehouses were centers of news and gossip. People gathered in them to play games, listen to music, and discuss the matters of the day. The conversations often turned to politics, and sometimes, when too many dangerous ideas were being discussed, the government or religious leaders shut the places down. But any ban on coffee and coffeehouses never lasted very long. Caffeine had already captured too many human minds.

Many religious and ethnic groups existed within the Ottoman Empire, but its rulers were Muslims. As coffee's defenders rightly pointed out, although Islam prohibits the drinking of alcohol, the religion has no rules against coffee. Coffee was seen as an acceptable alternative to wine and spirits. It became known by the Turkish word *kahve,* which, loosely translated, means "wine of Arabia." When the drink arrived in Europe, "kahve" became "coffee."

The Age of Caffeine

The Islamic world at this time was in many respects more advanced than Europe. Islamic scholars made great advances in mathematics, astronomy, and technology. For example, algebra was invented by Muslim mathematicians living in what is present-day Iran. The word *algebra* comes from Arabic.

Was coffee responsible for these scientific advances? Was it focusing the minds of the astronomers and mathematicians of the Muslim world? That is possible but difficult to prove. Yet the fact is that when tea drinking became popular in China, they too experienced a golden age of invention and thought. And, as it turns out, a similar thing happened when caffeine arrived in Europe.

Hard as it is to imagine, Europe had no coffee, tea, or chocolate until the 1600s. They all arrived around the same time, though they traveled from different directions. Tea came from Asia, coffee from North Africa and the Middle East, while chocolate came from Central America, brought by Spanish conquerors. The arrival of these caffeine-loaded drinks changed Europe by changing the European mind.

In Europe, unlike in the Ottoman Empire, alcohol was widely consumed in large amounts. People drank beer, wine, or spirits at every meal. They did so in part because alcoholic drinks were safer than water. Alcohol killed bacteria that might be in the water supply. People in the 1500s did not know about the link between microbes and disease, but they knew that alcohol was safer than water.

The switch from alcohol to coffee and tea, or at least the addition of coffee and tea to the daily routine, created a dramatic change in the mental state of Europeans. It helped people stay awake, and so changed the rhythm of their day. And once caffeine had captured the European mind, they of course wanted more of it.

Before Starbucks

When European travelers in Constantinople saw people drinking coffee, they were amazed. Drinking a hot beverage was unheard of in Europe. A Venetian wrote home in 1585 that the locals "are in the habit of drinking in public in shops and in the streets, a black liquid, boiling as they can stand it, which is extracted from a seed they call Cave . . . and is said to have the property of keeping a man awake."

The fact that you need to boil water to make coffee and tea meant they were the safest things a person could drink. They were even safer to drink than alcohol. Also, both coffee and tea contain chemicals called tannins that can kill microbes. Again, the Europeans did not understand the science, but drinking boiled beverages made them healthier.

The first coffeehouses in Europe popped up in Venice, Italy. They were modeled after the ones travelers had seen in Turkey, Egypt, and across North Africa. The first coffeehouse in England was opened in Oxford in 1650 by a Jewish immigrant named

Jacob. (What his last name was is not recorded.) Coffeehouses arrived in London soon after that and spread like a viral video. Within a few decades there were thousands of them in London.

In Europe, as in the Islamic world, coffee was mainly consumed in those coffeehouses. They were exciting meeting places where the news of the day was loudly discussed and debated. They were also democratic public spaces. In England they were the only place where men of different classes could mix. Anyone could sit anywhere. (Well, any *men*. Women were not welcome in either taverns or coffeehouses.) And compared to taverns, coffeehouses were polite and civil. If you started an argument, you were expected to buy a round for everyone.

These rooms served as the Internet of their time. A coffeehouse was where Londoners went to get news and information, rumor and gossip. Books, newspapers, and magazines were freely shared. You paid a penny for the coffee, but the information was free. For this reason, coffeehouses were often referred to as "penny universities."

Free Speech and Free Thought

London's coffeehouses served as clubs for men of various professions. For example, merchants and men in the shipping trade gathered at Lloyd's Coffee House. There they could learn what ships were arriving and departing. They could also find a broker who would sell them an insurance policy on their cargo.

Lloyd's Coffee House eventually became the famous insurance company called Lloyd's of London. In the same way, the London Stock Exchange began with trades conducted at Jonathan's Coffee-House.

Scholars and scientists gathered at the Grecian coffeehouse. The famous scientists Isaac Newton and Edmund Halley debated physics and mathematics there. Meanwhile the literary set, poets and writers, gathered at Will's or at Button's. Customers moved from one house to another, carrying news and opinions with them.

The conversation in London's coffeehouses often turned to politics. The freedom of speech sometimes disturbed the government. In 1675, King Charles II decided that the places were dangerous centers for plotting rebellion and ordered them closed. But by then the coffeehouse was such a fixture of English daily life—and so many important Londoners were addicted to caffeine—that everyone simply ignored the king's order. Faced with massive disobedience, the king quietly backed down.

In France too, coffeehouses were centers of free speech and free thought. The French Revolution of 1789 was planned in the coffeehouses of Paris. One of the centers for the rebellion was the Cafe de Procope. (*Café* is French for coffee.) The mob that stormed the Bastille assembled in the Café de Foy.

The ideas that were traded and debated in Europe's coffeehouses were part of a great movement historians call the Enlightenment. Before the Enlightenment, most Europeans believed religious faith and the Bible were the only things necessary to understand the world. Enlightenment philosophers argued that reason, logic, and science were the keys to understanding.

The Enlightenment gave rise to new inventions like the telescope and microscope. New methods of thought in economics, politics, and philosophy changed how people viewed society and government. The ideas that formed the foundation of the American Revolution were argued first in the coffeehouses of Europe. Writers including Daniel Defoe (*Robinson Crusoe*) and Jonathan Swift (*Gulliver's Travels*) took the informal language they heard in the coffeehouses and put it on the page for the first time, changing English literature.

Was it an accident that this revolutionary search for clarity and the nature of reality happened under the influence of caffeine? Was coffee necessary for this new school of thought to emerge? Voltaire, an important French Enlightenment writer and philosopher, certainly thought so. He supposedly drank as many as seventy-two cups a day.

Life Without Caffeine

Meanwhile, despite Voltaire's example, I had chosen to take a different path, one with no caffeine.

After a few weeks, the feelings of withdrawal had lessened. I could once again think in a straight line and hold an idea in my head for more than two minutes. I could work on this chapter again! Yet I continued to feel like I was just slightly behind the curve, especially compared to coffee and tea drinkers. By the time I got to my third month after quitting, I felt like I was standing on a train platform, watching coffee drinkers through the window as they streaked by in speeding trains.

I missed the way caffeine used to order my day into a rhythm of energetic peaks and valleys, as the mental tide of caffeine ebbs and flows. The morning surge is a blessing, obviously, but there is also something comforting in the ebb tide of afternoon, which a cup of tea can gently reverse.

I also missed the whole culture of coffee drinking—the smells and sounds of the coffee shop, sitting in a café and taking in the scene. Sure, I could sit among the coffee drinkers who are busy tapping away at their laptops, but it's not the same. I no longer shared their energy, their fierce concentration.

There were benefits to life without caffeine. I slept like a teenager again, and woke feeling refreshed, not groggy and needing a fix. I also found myself feeling proud of my caffeine fast, as if it showed some great strength of character. I no longer felt like I was being controlled by coffee. I no longer had to plan my day around my next fix. I was no longer a coffee addict. Instead of envying the customers in a coffee shop, I now pitied them.

And yet, I still missed my morning buzz.

I began to wonder if by giving up caffeine, I really had lost some mental ability. If a mental giant like Isaac Newton had used coffee, who was I to disagree? Or was the benefit of caffeine all in my imagination? After all, since caffeine improves your mood, maybe it didn't really make me smarter, it just made me feel more confident. Maybe I really was better off without it, without all the ups and downs.

Your Brain on Caffeine

I realized I was in no position to figure this out by myself. I decided to seek out scientific proof. Does caffeine really help you think? The answer is yes, *sort of*. Caffeine doesn't make you smarter, but it helps your brain to focus.

As we saw with bees, caffeine improves memory. Experiments show that subjects given caffeine after learning new material remembered it better. Caffeine also sharpens your physical skills. It improves physical performance in terms of speed, muscle strength, and endurance. (It also makes you go to the bathroom. Caffeine is a diuretic, which means it draws water out of your system, making you urinate. It's also a laxative, which means it helps you move your bowels.)

But those benefits of physical and mental performance come at a cost. One of the most serious is loss of sleep. The way caffeine works is by disrupting the body's sleep cycle. All day long, our bodies produce a chemical called adenosine. It's a tiny molecule that fits neatly into areas on brain cells called receptors. As the day goes by, more and more adenosine binds with nerve cells, and you feel increasingly sleepy. That is what's supposed to happen. The adenosine slows your brain so you can sleep. Then while you're asleep the adenosine is broken down by your body. You wake up feeling refreshed.

Caffeine is a tiny molecule that happens to fit snugly into the same nerve receptors as adenosine. It blocks adenosine from binding with your brain cells. The result is that you don't feel sleepy. How did plants happen to produce a chemical that is shaped just like adenosine? Through the random chance of evolution.

With caffeine blocking the way, your brain no longer receives a signal to begin slowing down. Even though more adenosine is still being produced, you don't feel its effects. Instead, you feel wide-awake and alert. But only temporarily. The adenosine is still there, its levels rising. When the caffeine wears off, the adenosine hits you all at once. You experience a crash.

Besides blocking adenosine, caffeine affects your brain in other ways. For example, it increases production of the chemical dopamine. Dopamine is very important for regulating your moods. More dopamine in your system can make you feel optimistic and happy. But when dopamine drops, your mood drops too.

Addictive and illegal drugs like cocaine greatly increase dopamine in your body. On those drugs, your brain quickly gets used to higher levels of the chemical. This is what happens to drug addicts. When those dopamine levels fall, they experience extreme distress and cravings for more. Stopping for an addict, especially all at once, can be dangerous.

We speak about coffee addiction, but it really isn't the same as addiction to drugs like heroin or cocaine. The addictive effects of coffee are much milder. Yes, you might crave another cup, but as my experience (and millions of others') shows, you can safely quit without too much discomfort.

Caffeine and Sleep

Is coffee bad for you? Until recently most doctors would have said yes, it is. When I was a kid, I was told that coffee would stunt my growth. Adults were told it increases blood pressure and can lead to heart attacks. Today, scientists and doctors know this simply isn't true. (Caffeine does temporarily raise your blood pressure but seems to have no long-term ill effects on your heart.)

In fact, research now shows that coffee and tea can be good for you. Notice I said coffee and tea, not caffeine. Other chemicals in coffee and tea are the healthy ones. They can decrease your risk of some types of cancer and help prevent heart disease and diabetes. But you can get all those benefits by drinking decaffeinated tea or coffee.

Caffeine, on the other hand, may be bad for your health because it interferes with sleep. As we've seen, it displaces adenosine in your brain and interrupts your natural sleep cycle. In the modern age, we tend to take sleep for granted. After all, we can turn on the lights, or the computer screen, at any hour of the day or night. People brag about how little sleep they need, or about "pulling an all-nighter" before a big test.

Like many of us, I'd never thought about sleep much, until I talked with Matt Walker, a scientist at University of California,

Berkeley. Walker wrote a book on the subject, *Why We Sleep*. It's one of the scarier books I've read. It argues that caffeine itself might not be bad for you, but the sleep it's stealing from you could be bad for your health.

I met with Walker while doing research for this chapter. He's a compact and wired man—I would describe him as caffeinated except that I know he is not. Although he grew up in England drinking black tea every morning, he no longer consumes caffeine in any form. In fact, none of the sleep researchers I interviewed for this chapter use caffeine. Maybe that should tell us something.

Walker is single-minded in his mission: to alert the world to an invisible public-health crisis. It is, he says, a crisis of not enough sleep. According to Walker, lack of sleep may be a key factor in the development of Alzheimer's disease, heart disease, stroke, depression, anxiety, suicide, and obesity. "The shorter you sleep," he bluntly concludes, "the shorter your life span."

I told you it was scary. If Walker is correct, poor sleep is a worldwide health crisis, and one of the main causes of this crisis is caffeine.

Deep Sleep

I'd thought of myself as a pretty good sleeper before I met Matt Walker. At lunch he asked me about my sleep habits. I told him I usually get a solid seven hours, fall asleep easily, and dream most nights.

He told me that the amount of time you sleep is only part of the story. How well you sleep is just as important for your health. If you get up several times a night or don't sleep soundly, you will miss out on one of the most important parts of the sleep cycle: "deep" or "slow-wave" sleep.

You may have heard of REM sleep. (*REM* stands for rapid eye movement.) REM sleep is when you dream. Slow-wave or deep sleep is a different stage of the sleep cycle. During deep sleep, low-frequency electric pulses move through the brain. These waves organize the many thoughts, feelings, and experiences that have built up during the day. Long-term memories are formed while less important things are forgotten. It's as if the mental desktop is being cleared off and reorganized at the end of the school day.

Walker explained that even if you manage to fall asleep with no problem, the caffeine you had earlier in the day may be harming your deep sleep. Even after twelve hours, about one-quarter of the caffeine you drank is still in your system. That means, if you have a cup of coffee at two p.m., there's still about a quarter of a cup in your brain at two a.m. That could well be enough to completely wreck your deep sleep.

"Some people say they can drink coffee at night and fall right to sleep," Walker told me, with a note of pity in his voice. "That might be the case, but the amount of slow-wave sleep they get will still drop by fifteen to twenty percent."

Caffeine is not the sole cause of our sleep crisis. Looking at phone or computer screens can disrupt sleep, as can prescription drugs, noise and light pollution, and anxiety. But caffeine is at or near the top of the list.

Walker says, "If you plot the rise in the number of Starbucks coffeehouses over the past thirty-five years and the rise in sleep loss over that period, the lines look very similar."

Here's what's really strange about our caffeine use: It's the leading cause of our sleep loss, and at the same time, it's the main tool we use to make up for sleep loss. Caffeine helps hide the very problem that caffeine creates.

Charles Czeisler, an expert on sleep rhythms at Harvard Medical School, put it this way: "We use caffeine to make up for sleep loss that is largely the result of using caffeine."

When I spoke to Czeisler, he told me he doesn't use caffeine either.

Caffeine seems to be a source of human energy, but there is no free lunch: It is simply hiding or postponing our exhaustion by blocking the action of adenosine. As the body breaks down the caffeine, all that built-up adenosine floods the brain and you crash, feeling even more tired than you did before that first cup of coffee. So what will you do then? Probably have another cup.

Hooked on Caffeine

Young people are full of energy, but the fact is they need more sleep than older people. Teenagers and kids need deep sleep more than adults to help their brains develop. That's why it really is a good idea to limit your caffeine use to small amounts early in the day. But here's another trick caffeine plays on us. After you use it for a while, it doesn't work as well. You have to drink more coffee or tea to get the same boost of energy.

Drinking coffee, it's easy to get caught in a cycle. You use caffeine to wake up, it wears off, you have to drink more to stay awake, and then you need even more because it doesn't work as well. The caffeine stays in your system and you don't sleep well, so you wake up and need . . . more caffeine.

Why do companies put caffeine in soft drinks, especially in drinks marketed to kids? The soft drink industry has claimed that the caffeine is there as a flavoring. Really? Laboratory tests have proven that most people can't taste the difference between drinks with caffeine and those without. And yet, the six top-selling soda brands in the United States all contain caffeine (typically about as much as in a cup of tea). Why?

Remember the experiment that Geraldine Wright did with bees? The bees developed a preference for nectar that had been caffeinated—even when they couldn't taste it. The caffeine helped them remember the other flavors in the nectar. It drove them to want more, *even when it wasn't good for them*. The soda makers have figured out what the plants learned to do a long time ago. They add caffeine to their sugar water to keep us coming back.

What should kids do about caffeine? As a once and future caffeine user, I will not lecture anyone to give it up. But I will tell you from my own experience and from the research I did for this chapter, caffeine is a powerful drug. Loss of sleep is a serious problem, especially for young people. So if you are going to have coffee or tea, or any caffeinated drinks, be smart about it. Caffeine is in all sorts of drinks, where you might not expect it. Be aware of what you're drinking and limit your intake.

Stolen Mocha

Even when coffee was first introduced to Europe, there were some who opposed the beverage. Medical men debated whether it was healthy. Women, who were not welcome in the coffeehouses, objected to the amount of time their husbands spent there. These protests fell on deaf ears. Caffeine had already taken hold of the European mind.

But owners of European coffeehouses had a problem. Arab traders had an absolute monopoly on coffee beans. They made a profit on every cup of coffee consumed in London, Paris, or Amsterdam. It was a monopoly they carefully guarded. Coffee beans are seeds. If you plant one under the right conditions, you can grow a coffee bush. To make sure this never happened, the Arab merchants roasted their beans before they shipped them, killing the tiny plants in each seed.

Then, in 1616 a sneaky Dutchman managed to smuggle live coffee plants out of Mocha, a port city of Yemen. (Which is where the term *mocha* comes from.) He took the plants to the botanical garden in Amsterdam, where they were grown in a greenhouse. The Dutch made cuttings of the plants and rooted them in soil. Soon they had several identical coffee bushes.

Some of them were sent to a Dutch colony, the Indonesian island of Java. The Dutch East India Company successfully started growing coffee plants, eventually producing enough to establish a plantation there. And so, the stolen coffee grown in the Dutch colony was called Mocha Java.

In 1714, two offspring of the Dutchman's stolen coffee bush were given to King Louis XIV, of France. He had it planted in the royal greenhouses in Paris. A few years later, a former French naval officer named Gabriel de Clieu decided to try growing coffee in the French colony of Martinique in the Caribbean, where he lived. He claimed to have gotten a woman in the royal palace to steal a cutting of the king's plant—another coffee theft.

After successfully rooting the cutting, de Clieu put the little plant in a glass box to protect it from the elements and brought it with him on a ship bound for Martinique. The crossing took much longer than planned and the travelers ran low on water. Determined to keep his coffee plant alive, de Clieu shared his small allowance of water with it.

De Clieu claimed to have nearly died of thirst at sea, but his sacrifice ensured that the plant made it safely to Martinique. There, the stolen plant thrived. By 1730, France's Caribbean colonies were shipping coffee back to Europe. Much of the coffee grown in the Americas today are descendants of that original plant smuggled out of Mocha in 1616.

Ready to Work

By 1730, the changes coffee had made in European society were very clear. As early as 1660, writer and historian James Howell wrote that apprentices and clerks used to start their day with ale or wine, which made them unfit for business. But now they drank coffee and were wide-awake and ready to work.

Long before the coffee break, there was the beer break. Most labor was physical, not mental, and much of it took place outdoors, on farmland, or carrying and hauling goods from one place to another. Workers didn't need to be mentally sharp or pay attention to clocks. (Most people didn't have one.)

But in the mid-1700s, with the start of the Industrial Revolution in Europe, the nature of work began to change. For laborers working with machines, a mind dulled by alcohol was a safety hazard and a drag on productivity. For clerks and others who worked with numbers, wine and beer in the morning made accurate work very difficult. Coffee provided the exact drug needed for this new age. It focused the mind just when more and more people depended on their minds to make a living.

Did coffee make the Industrial Revolution possible, or did it merely show up at exactly the right time to help it? Surely it can't be a coincidence that coffee and the minute hand on clocks arrived at more or less the same moment. People in the Middle Ages had no need of a clock. If you're working outside in a field, all you have to do is look at the angle of the sun to know how much daylight is left. If you're working your own plot of land, you decide how much you can or want to do in the daylight that is left. You measure the day in large chunks—morning, afternoon, evening.

But clerks in an office or workers in a factory needed a new way of measuring the day. First of all, they had to get to work on time. They had to stay until it was time to quit. They got paid according to the work they did in the hours in between. Their employers needed to know how much was being produced every hour. For those workers, and their bosses, minutes became a necessity. Caffeine was the ideal drug to help everyone focus on the advancing minutes of the day.

Who Needs Sunlight?

Much more revolutionary was the way caffeine made it possible for people to ignore the sun altogether. The sun, after all, is the original clock. Our bodies evolved to follow its rhythms, to be awake when the sun is up and go to sleep when it's down. Before caffeine, the whole idea of a late shift, let alone a night shift, was unnatural. The human body simply would not permit it.

Caffeine made it possible to ignore our bodies' natural clocks. With the aid of oil lamps, gas lighting, and eventually electric lights, and fueled by caffeine, factories could now operate twenty-four hours a day. Maybe coffee didn't cause the Industrial

Revolution, but it's hard to imagine this great change in work and life without it.

In previous chapters, we looked at an equal partnership between the apple and the tulip and humanity. Both sides could be seen to benefit. Coffee and tea present a different, more complicated picture. Has humanity really benefited from this partnership or has our thirst for caffeine made life worse?

Caffeine, by cutting our ties to the natural rhythm of our bodies, freed us in many ways. It made it possible to live life 24/7, with all the joys and stresses that brings. It meant we could enjoy a night life, but also that we might never get enough sleep. It sped us up so we could keep pace with machines and now the never-sleeping Internet. But it made it possible to never unplug.

Is this good or bad or a little of both? These are questions that are debated by scholars, philosophers, scientists, and perhaps even people sitting around in coffee shops. The answers go far beyond the scope of this book, but they are certainly worth thinking about.

Tea and coffee hit upon the secret of making caffeine by chance, then over millions of years, they developed a partnership with bees and other pollinators. Then, also by chance, human beings discovered the power of caffeine. Our partnership with the plants is an accident of history. No one made a decision to let caffeine into our lives; it more or less forced its way in. After just a few hundred years, it's hard to predict how this partnership will end up. Perhaps the best we can hope for is that caffeine will help us cope with the problems that caffeine created.

The Human Cost of Caffeine

The history of humans, tea, and coffee has an uglier side. Europeans craved caffeine so much, they were willing to commit terrible crimes against other people to get it.

We think of the British as tea drinkers, but at first, coffee was much more popular in England. Tea was more expensive and only the upper classes could afford it. It wasn't until the late 1700s, when British East India Company began trading regularly with China, that the price of tea came down. By the year 1800, tea was being consumed daily by just about everyone in England.

English workers, driven into the cities by the Industrial Revolution, relied on tea to get through long shifts, brutal working conditions, and more or less constant hunger. Caffeine in tea helped quiet the hunger pangs, and the sugar added to it was an important source of calories.

In China, tea was never sweetened. Adding sugar to it seems to be a British invention. No one knows exactly why it started, but the tea imported by Great Britain tended to be bitter. Perhaps sugar was necessary to make it drinkable. Since the beverage was hot, it could absorb large amounts of sugar. As tea grew in popularity, so did the demand for sugar. By the 1800s, one of the main uses of sugar in Britain was for sweetening tea.

Where did the sugar come from? It came from plantations on British colonies in the West Indies, plantations run with enslaved laborers. In fact, the demand for sugar helped expand the slave trade. African people were stolen from their homes and jammed into ships in chains to cross the Atlantic. Untold millions died on the voyage from illness or starvation, and their bodies were dumped at sea.

Once in British colonies, these people were sold as property and subjected to brutal whippings, beatings, and torture to force them to grow sugarcane. Coffee was also grown by enslaved laborers in the West Indies and also in Brazil. This was of course the same system of slave labor that brought Africans to the British colonies that became the United States.

Sugar from the West Indies was also made into molasses, which was in turn made into rum. This formed one corner of the so-called Triangle Trade. Ships brought enslaved people from Africa to the Americas. The same ships brought rum and sugar to England. From there the same ships returned to Africa for a new cargo of human beings. Many merchants in New York and Boston became wealthy from this evil exchange.

Did tea and coffee drinkers in Europe have any idea that their caffeine and sugar habits came from such brutality? At least some did. In 1820, an English woman named Elizabeth Heyrick started a boycott of sugar as a protest against slavery. Many other abolitionists (people who wanted to end, or abolish, slavery) joined in.

Opium for Tea

While sugar bore the ugly stain of slavery, its partner, tea, had a moral stain of another kind. Most tea in Britain came from China, but the Chinese had little interest in trading for British goods. That meant the British East India Company had to pay for tea with gold or silver, something the British government did not want to do.

The East India Company decided to turn the British colony of India into a producer of two crops it had never grown before—tea and opium. Opium, which is highly addictive and dangerous, is another plant-produced drug. It's made from sap of the poppy flower.

The Indian tea was exported to England, but the opium was smuggled into China, where it was traded for more tea. By 1828, the opium trade represented 16 percent of the East India Company's revenues. Within five years, it was sending more than five million pounds of Indian opium to China per year. So here was another cost of caffeine: In order for the English mind to be sharpened by tea, the Chinese mind had to be clouded by opium.

Opium was illegal in China and the Chinese government tried to stop the British from bringing it into their country. Millions of Chinese people became addicted, which helped to bring down the Chinese economy. In 1839, the Chinese emperor ordered the seizure of all stores of opium and, in response, Britain declared war to keep the opium flowing. Thanks to its navy's vastly superior firepower, Britain won. They forced the Chinese government to open five Chinese cities to European control. They also took ownership of Hong Kong, which they held until 1997.

These stories from history are terrible and shocking. But we have to ask ourselves, do we know any more about the system that produces our coffee and tea than consumers did during the time of slavery or the Opium Wars? The supply chain that delivers us our daily dose of caffeine is largely invisible. While it no longer rests on the backs of enslaved people or those addicted to opium, it still relies on vast inequality.

Coffee and tea are grown in Africa, Asia, or Latin America, but much of it is consumed in Europe or the United States. Coffee sales in the United States alone reach almost fifteen billion dollars a year. Very little of that vast sum ever reaches the people who produce the beans. For every four-dollar latte, only a few pennies go to the farmers who grow the beans, most of whom work a few mountainous acres in some rural corner of a tropical country. Of the ten dollars you might pay for a pound of coffee, only about one dollar reaches the farmer who grew it.

Over the years, coffee-growing countries have tried to band together to get a good price for their products. But they've been overpowered by the strength of large international corporations and buyers who trade on markets in London or New York, driving prices down to the lowest possible point. In many years, farmers are forced to sell their beans for less than what it cost to grow them.

A handful of companies like Starbucks and nonprofits like Fairtrade International have tried to guarantee that coffee farmers get a fair share of the profits. But they are up against an international system that favors the big buyers while keeping the farmers in poverty.

The First Cup

The time came to wrap up my experiment in quitting caffeine. I had learned what I could and enjoyed a great number of excellent nights' sleep. I was eager to see how my caffeine-free body would react to a couple shots of espresso. I was ready to rejoin the human community of the caffeinated.

I had thought long and hard about where I'd go to enjoy my first cup. At first, I considered getting it from the Peet's in my neighborhood in Berkeley, California. The shop happens to be the original Peet's, founded in 1966. The store represents a turning point in American coffee drinking.

It was Alfred Peet, the son of a Dutch coffee roaster, who almost single-handedly introduced America to good coffee. Before Peet opened his shop, Americans drank diner coffee from blue-and-white cardboard cups, or they brewed it at home from cans of Folgers or Maxwell House. Most of this coffee was made from inferior robusta beans, which are high in caffeine but bitter and not very flavorful. But it was cheap, and it was all we knew.

Peet, who had tasted better in the Netherlands, insisted on using arabica beans and roasting them slowly, until they were quite dark. His exacting standards created the coffee culture in which we now live. A generous man, Peet taught a whole generation of American coffee roasters, including the founders of Starbucks, who worked for him at the Berkeley shop. Peet also taught Americans to pay a few dollars, rather than a quarter or two, for a cup of coffee. He transformed coffee drinking into the expensive habit is today.

But alas, I don't *love* Peet's coffee, and I decided to honor a more personal coffee tradition. I would go to the Cheese Board, a bakery-café where Judith and I have been morning regulars for many years. I'd get a special, their term for a double-shot espresso drink made with steamed milk.

Out in front of the Cheese Board, a couple of parking spaces have been converted into a sweet little pocket park. It contains a few benches, a couple of flower planters and trees, and a thick wooden counter to lean on. I seldom take the time to hang out there, but this was a lovely midsummer Saturday morning. We decided to linger, finding a seat where we could enjoy our coffees and take in the scene. I sat down and had my first sip.

My special was *unbelievably* good, a ringing reminder of what I'd been missing. It held depths of flavor I had completely forgotten about! I could almost feel the tiny molecules of caffeine spreading through my body and slipping into my brain to plug into my adenosine receptors.

Well-being was the term that best described that first feeling. The sensation built and spread until I decided *joy* was the right word. It wasn't the usual feeling of the first cup in the morning, which is a return to normal as the fog of caffeine withdrawal lifts. This first cup was much, much stronger. It gave me a whole new way of looking at the world.

I looked around me, taking in the moms with kids in their strollers, and the dogs trailing them for crumbs. Everything seemed better, sharper, more *real*. I wondered if all these people with their cardboard cups had any idea what a powerful drug they were sipping. But how could they? They had long ago gotten used to caffeine. They used it to keep from feeling rotten—to feel *normal*. They could no longer use it to feel *great*.

The Voice of Caffeine

I realized that this wonderful feeling couldn't last. In just a few days' time, I too would get used to the effects of caffeine. Then the only way to feel this boost would be to drink even more, with an even greater crash waiting for me. How could I preserve coffee's effects? Only by using it less. Maybe I could think of coffee like a treat and just drink it on Saturdays?

After about half an hour, I could feel my surge of joy wearing off. A garbage truck had pulled across the street. The mechanical arms began to lift tall plastic garbage bins and dump them. The racket was unbearable—or so I felt. Then I realized it was the coffee, making me super sensitive. I felt every molecule making me hyperaware and full of energy—to do something, anything.

I went home and started doing something I'd never done on my own. I decided to clean out my closet. Suddenly, I wanted nothing more than to take all my sweaters off the shelf and sort them into piles. Ordinarily, I have a hard time throwing anything out. But with caffeine urging me on, I was merciless. I quickly filled a large garbage bag of sweaters, sneakers, and shirts to give away or throw out.

The morning went on like that. I got a lot done. In the garden

I raked, I weeded, I put things in order. Whatever I focused on, I focused on single-mindedly. I was like a horse wearing blinders. I could sink myself into a task and fail to notice that an hour had passed.

Around noon, the energy began to subside, and I decided on a new task. I decided to go to the garden center to buy some new plants. It was during the drive that I realized the true reason I was heading to that particular garden center: They had an Airstream trailer parked out front that served really good espresso drinks!

I had only had a single cup of coffee after three months, and already it had sunk its tentacles into my brain. What had happened to my resolution to drink coffee only on Saturday? Then I heard a voice say, "But it's *still Saturday!*" I knew immediately who it was: It was the voice of caffeine. It took all the willpower I had to resist it.

The Home of Juan Valdez

Partway through my research for this chapter, it occurred to me that I should go see how coffee was grown and meet some of the people who grew it.

Judith and I traveled to Medellín, Colombia, a city that's the gateway to Colombia's coffee-growing region. On a January morning, we hired a car to take us up into the mountains south of the city. Our destination was Café de la Cima, a coffee farm, or *finca*.

We traveled along rutted dirt roads outside of Fredonia, a lively little market town, and along the way we passed Cerro Tusa, a green triangle of a volcano.

Cerro Tusa is the same mountain that is on the logo for the Colombian coffee growers' association. It appears on every package of their beans and in TV commercials for Colombian coffee. On the logo, standing in front of Cerro Tusa, is Juan Valdez, a Colombian campesino, or peasant farmer. He is leading his faithful burro, Conchita.

Juan has been appearing in ads for Colombian coffee since 1958. He's been able to have such a long career because he doesn't really exist. Juan Valdez is a purely fictional person. He was born in the brain of an advertising copywriter in a New York ad agency. He's been played by several actors over the years.

Octavio Acevedo and his son Humberto, the owners of Café de la Cima, could easily play Juan Valdez on TV. They fit the part right down to the straw hat and colorful serape. Humberto, who showed us around the seven-acre finca, is the fourth generation to grow coffee on this steep, lush hillside. But the operation has changed in important ways since his grandfather farmed it.

"Five years ago," Humberto explained as we set out to visit his shrubs, "my father decided he wanted to taste the coffee he was growing." This was an unusual idea; most campesinos sell their coffee to middlemen while the beans are still "green"—freshly picked and unprocessed. If they drink coffee at all, it's coffee grown by someone else and is probably the drink called *tinto*. That's the thick, concentrated coffee made from cheap beans that most Colombians still drink. All the best beans go to the United States or Europe.

But Octavio could see there was no future for a small farmer selling beans in a global market. His beans got mixed in with all the similar beans grown in Colombia. He needed a brand—a reason for consumers to seek out his coffee. He decided he wouldn't just grow coffee beans; he'd clean, ferment, dry, and roast them on his farm. Café de la Cima would become a brand known for its quality. His finca would become a destination for people like me, curious to see where and how their coffee is produced.

Hard Work Harvesting

Humberto was eager to introduce us to the twelve thousand coffee plants with whom the family shares the green, sun-drenched hillside. Café de la Cima is perched 1,600 meters (about one mile) above sea level. Coffee likes tropical mountains because the plant needs both a lot of rain and well-drained soil. The mountain slopes allow excess water to drain away. The high elevation also allows coffee to escape one of its most destructive pests, a fungus called coffee leaf rust.

But climate change is already pushing coffee production higher up the mountain and making life difficult for farmers. Coffee plants are notoriously picky about rainfall, temperature, and sunlight, all of which are changing in Colombia. Lands that had always been good for coffee production no longer have the right temperature or rainfall. Thanks to climate change, the future for global coffee production is growing increasingly grim. By one estimate, roughly half of the world's coffee-growing acreage will be useless by 2050.

Humberto led us up a steep path behind the house. We passed a nursery where he was sprouting coffee plants—dozens of tiny seedlings. In the past, the Acevedos would have bought new plants to replace the ones that were too old to produce anymore. Now they grow their own, selecting seeds (beans) from the best plants on their farm. That way they grow plants that are better suited for their own small patch of ground.

Up past the nursery, we crossed a little stream and stepped into the first row of coffee plants. The five-foot-tall shrubs were planted in curving parallel lines. Each was carefully pruned and had slender branches lined with glossy green leaves and beans. Most of the young coffee fruit was still green, but there were a handful of bright red ones that looked like cranberries. Humberto handed Judith and me each a basket, called a *fanega,* which is worn in front at waist height and suspended by a strap over the shoulder.

He shooed us away: *Go pick some coffee!*

We each went our own way, stepping gingerly down a different narrow row of spiky green shrubs. The hillside was so steep, I had to carefully sidestep my way from plant to plant. I bent over and reached through the leaves to pick only the reddest cherries, one by one, and dropped them in my basket. I bit into a ripe red one. The flesh tasted fruity and sweet, with just a hint of coffee flavor, and in the center sat a small tan seed, divided into two lobes. That was the coffee bean.

Humberto had told me it takes fifty or so coffee beans to make a single cup of coffee. After a half hour of picking, I had collected enough beans for maybe four or five cups. Already my back and feet were screaming with pain. During the harvest season, which lasts three months, coffee pickers work ten to twelve hours a day picking coffee cherries. The workers are usually migrants who have traveled from other parts of Colombia or other countries just for the harvest. They're paid by the number of fanegas they can fill. A skilled picker will make twenty dollars a day; an unskilled one as little as five dollars. We were getting just a tiny taste of what that work must be like.

It was hard to believe that coffee was still picked that way, by hand, bean by bean, as it has been for centuries. The steep slopes make it hard to use machinery or combine fincas. The biggest change at Café de la Cima is the one that has put Conchita the donkey out of work. When a picker's basket is full, they no longer strap it to the back of a burro for the ride down the hillside. Now they spill the basket of coffee cherries into a concrete box at the top of the hill. A stream of well water then flushes the cherries through a steel pipe, carrying them down the mountain and directly into the processing shed.

I didn't pick enough coffee to fill my basket, not even close. One problem was I had to stretch my legs and straighten up every few minutes, or my back would ache terribly. The hillside was so steep, and the rows so tightly planted, that it was difficult to find a place to stand. I felt off-balance the entire time, which made it hard to work. Among the coffee shrubs, in their habitat, I felt like an interloper, out of place.

A Success Story?

I stepped out of the row I'd been working and gazed out over the Andes Mountains. One green ridge overlapped another, each covered with rows of shiny green coffee plants. Whatever had grown there originally had long been displaced by coffee, helped by humans like the Acevedos who were answering the demand of other humans around the planet.

You couldn't tell by looking at it, but this sleepy rural scene was deeply connected to our urban lives. One doesn't exist without the other. The two communities are tied together, driven by our desire for the taste for coffee. That desire has transformed the mountains of Colombia along with landscapes across Latin America and Africa and Asia. At the same time, it has transformed the lives of billions of people living in cities around the globe.

Yet, as we've seen, it's not coffee's taste that worked those changes. It's the tiny molecule in the drink, and what that molecule did for us once it found its way into our brains. The plants have turned the mountainsides into factories for the production of caffeine. All the glossy green leaves transform the rays of the tropical sun and the nutrients in the soils into 1,3,7-trimethylxanthine—the chemical we know as caffeine. It's hard to imagine that this unhurried and peaceful landscape produces so much speed, energy, and activity in the rest of the world.

You really have to give the plant a lot of credit. In less than a thousand years it has managed to get itself from its birthplace in Ethiopia all the way to the mountains of South America and beyond. It used human beings to accomplish all of that. Consider all we've done on this plant's behalf. We set aside more than twenty-seven million acres of new habitat. We employed twenty-five million humans to carefully tend it. We bid up its price until it became one of the most precious crops on earth.

This is a strange partnership, one very different from other partnerships we have with plants. Coffee and tea have not only benefited by gratifying human desire, they've helped create a world of nonstop industry, urban life, global trade, twenty-four-hour lifestyles, all run by people who by now can barely get out of bed without their help. It's a world that seems tailor-made for coffee and tea, and a world that, to a great extent, coffee and tea helped create.

Once again, we have to ask the question: Who is really in charge? Are we using coffee and tea, or are they using us? We naturally assume we're the boss in this arrangement. But perhaps that's just the voice of caffeine in our brains. Who has really benefited the most? Have our partnerships with coffee and tea been bad or good for the human race, or a little of both? These are questions that remain to be answered. What do you think?

My own relationship to caffeine remains a work in progress. I've been trying to keep to the pledge I made and reserve it for special occasions. For several weeks I drank caffeinated coffee only on Saturdays. Of course, this so dramatically improved my Saturdays that I gradually found myself slipping in a little caffeine during the week. Every now and then, I'd have a cup of green tea. As with so many addictions, the slope is slippery; the mind makes up clever arguments for just one more sip, one more cup.

When Judith and I walk down the hill to the Cheese Board each morning, I am always unsure what I'll order right up to the moment when I step to the front of the line. It takes all my strength to resist saying to the barista:

"Make it a regular, please."

Chapter Four

Desire: *Control*

Plant: *The Potato*

To my eye, there are few sights in nature quite as stirring as fresh rows of vegetable seedlings rising like a green city on the spring ground. I love the visual rhythm of new green plants and black earth. In early spring everything is neat and orderly, before the weeds take over, before the pests hit the plants, and before the vines and leaves have overgrown my small plot.

That is the moment when I can enjoy the illusion that I have arranged everything perfectly, that it's all under my control. That illusion vanishes as the spring turns into summer and then fall. Even in my small garden, even with a lot of effort, things just don't turn out exactly the way I'd planned. Sooner or later, it's clear that nature is in control, as it always is and always has been.

No one understands this more than farmers, whose success depends on so many things beyond their control, starting with the weather. Every spring they plant their crops, sure of only one thing—that they can't be sure of anything. Will the rain arrive to make the seeds sprout? Will there be too much rain? Will disease kill off the plants before they can bear fruit? They're in a constant struggle with the forces of nature.

Just outside of Paris stands the palace of Versailles, once home to King Louis XVI and Marie Antoinette. The large, carefully designed gardens there were planted centuries ago. They're a wonderful example of an attempt to bring nature under our control. Everything is laid out in straight lines, including the carefully pruned trees and shrubs. But in December 1999, a freak windstorm fueled by climate change laid waste to many of the plantings that had stood for generations. Overnight, nature reasserted its power.

Whenever I think I have things under control in my garden, I remember what happened to the gardens at Versailles.

Changing the Balance

In previous chapters, we looked at partnerships between humans and plants. We saw that those partnerships represent a sort of balance—the apple gave humans sweetness, the tulip gave us beauty, and in return we helped them spread and thrive. In the case of coffee and tea, we saw that those plants, by producing caffeine and altering our behavior, have shifted the balance of the partnership. They control us in ways we don't fully understand.

In this chapter, I want to look at how we are changing the partnership between humans and plants in ways that have never been done before. We are no longer merely forming *partnerships* with plants; we're changing their environment, going to war with their pests, and killing the soil they grow in. We've begun to change the very essence of some plants, tinkering with their genes to create organisms that nature could never produce.

These developments amount to a radical change in our partnership with plants. They represent an attempt by people to once and for all overcome the power of nature and be in complete control of what happens on our farms and in our gardens.

I want to examine this change by looking at one of the most basic food crops on the planet, one you are probably very familiar with—the potato. The simple spud, mashed, baked, or deep fried, is comfort food for many of us. Yet we are changing the way it is grown, and we are changing the potato itself, in ways that may not be comforting at all.

To be clear, humans have been changing plants for thousands of years. We graft one type of apple tree onto another and cross-breed them to produce new varieties. We plant tulips we find beautiful (or easy to market) and let other types die out. We mix types of fruits to create the plumcot, the tangelo, and many more. We select and favor natural mutations like the nectarine, which is really a type of smooth-skinned peach.

The potato is a prime example of this. The wild potato is too bitter and toxic to eat. Centuries ago, people living in South America learned to select and breed potatoes that were tasty and wholesome. They did what people around the world have done for centuries—they took plants as they existed in nature, encouraged some traits, and ignored others.

In some ways, every garden is a place of experimentation. When we farm or garden, we clear the ground of the natural ecosystem and create a blank canvas. This makes space for us to try out new hybrids and varieties, including some that arrive by accident.

But in recent years, we've seen a new, bolder type of human experiment. Instead of working with the nature of plants, we've learned to change their genes. We've taken genes from one plant and put them into the genes of another. We've even taken DNA from other organisms like bacteria or fish and put them into plants.

These creations are called genetically modified organisms or GMOs, or sometimes bioengineered plants. In a very short span of time, GMOs have become a giant share of our food supply. While there aren't that many GMO crops, they make up a large percentage of some basic foods. Ninety-two percent of our corn is GMO, 94 percent of soy, 99.9 percent of sugar beets. Also, more than 95 percent of animals raised for meat and dairy in the United States eat GMO feed.

Chances are very good that you've been eating GMOs in one form or another.

My Plant Lab

In this chapter, I want to look at GMOs and other radical changes in the way we produce our food. I think it's important to do that with an open mind. As I said, experimentation has always been a part of our relationship with plants. Even in my own little garden, I'm constantly experimenting with new types of plants, methods of fertility, and pest control.

Admittedly, my garden experiments are unscientific. If there are fewer beetles on my potato plants, is it because of the neem-oil I sprayed on them? Or is it because the beetles prefer the leaves of the nearby tomatillos I planted to distract them? I can never be sure, but through trial and error my garden improves. I'm always ready to try something new.

That's why a few years ago I decided to experiment with something very new. I planted a potato called the "NewLeaf," a genetically modified organism (GMO). The Monsanto Corporation, which created the NewLeaf, promised it would revolutionize potato growing by killing the potato's number one enemy—the Colorado potato beetle. That's a handsome, extremely hungry insect that can pick a potato plant clean of its leaves overnight.

Before NewLeaf, farmers and gardeners fought the potato beetle with insecticides—chemicals that they sprayed on the leaves. But in a miracle of bioengineering, the NewLeaf potato makes its own insecticide. No spraying is necessary. It produces it in every cell of every leaf, stem, flower, root, and—this is the unsettling part—every spud.

Monsanto created this wonder of science by taking a gene from a common bacterium with the scientific name of *Bacillus thuringiensis,* or "Bt" for short. The Bt bacterium naturally produces a toxin that kills Colorado potato beetles. Bt toxin has been considered harmless to humans, and even organic farmers use it—by spraying it on their potato plants.

Working in a laboratory, scientists at Monsanto "snipped" the gene from the bacterium and inserted it in the DNA of a potato. With the code of that gene, the potato could now produce the same Bt toxin. Any Colorado potato beetle that takes so much as a nibble of a NewLeaf leaf is supposedly doomed.

I was interested in growing NewLeaf potatoes, but I wasn't sure I wanted to eat them. As I said, the inserted gene causes NewLeafs to produce Bt toxin in every part of the plant, including the fat tubers we eat. Of course, Monsanto insisted they were safe to eat, otherwise what would be the point of growing them? But could I rely on their word? After all, they had an awful lot of money at stake.

Scientists promise us that in the future, bioengineered plants will do even more wonderful things. They say we can have corn that can grow with less water or cotton that grows in every color of the rainbow. We can have potatoes that deliver vaccines or rice that is rich in Vitamin A.

These radically new plants sound wonderful but also unsettling. I'm all for using science to make our lives better, but how can we be sure these laboratory creations are truly safe? I knew that, like you, I'd most likely been eating GMO food for years without knowing it, but did I really want to eat a potato filled with bacterial insecticide if I didn't have to?

I decided to try to get some answers.

Who Owns My Potatoes?

Monsanto[1] and other big agribusiness corporations say that GMOs are pretty much the same as the potatoes, corn, and beans we've always eaten. But as soon as I began to plant my NewLeafs I discovered at least one startling difference. You know those long

---

[1]   In 2016, Monsanto was bought by Bayer, an international corporate giant based in Germany. My experiment with the NewLeaf potatoes took place several years before that.

legal documents that come with apps, the small print kind that you don't ever read, but just click on "I agree"? My potatoes came with one of those, except printed on paper.

Potatoes, you will recall from kindergarten experiments, are not grown from seeds but from the eyes of other potatoes. Monsanto had sent me a purple mesh bag of dusty, stone-colored potato chunks. After digging two shallow trenches in my vegetable garden and lining them with compost, I opened the bag and found the "grower's guide" tied to the opening.

By "opening and using this product," the card informed me, I was now "licensed" to grow these potatoes. That was strange. I'd never had a potato-growing license before—I'd never needed one. I owned these potatoes, the card went on, and any new potatoes that grew from them. I could eat them or sell them. But there was a catch. I was not allowed, by law, to save any of them to plant next spring. If I performed that simple act, something farmers and gardeners have been doing for thousands of years, I would be breaking federal law.

It turned out, as the card explained, that while I might own those potatoes, Monsanto owned their genes. This is a difficult idea to get your head around. Look at it this way. If you buy a smart phone, you own that phone. But you're not allowed to manufacture new copies of your phone. You own the phone but not the right to duplicate it.

Monsanto was saying the same logic applied to their potatoes. I owned them but couldn't make copies. The problem, of course, is that potatoes are living things, which naturally make their own

155

copies. That is the whole point of growing crops. What would happen, I wondered, if these potatoes sent off shoots that grew into new plants next spring? Gardeners call these "volunteers," plants that seed or spread on their own. Would federal marshals show up and arrest me?

I realized I had run smack into one of the biggest problems facing modern farmers. Over just a few generations, they've become completely dependent on big businesses like Monsanto. An American farmer today grows enough food each year to feed a hundred or more people. But they do it with large quantities of chemical fertilizers, pesticides, machinery, and fuel, all of which they must buy each year.

This is very different from the way farmers worked one hundred years ago. They might buy seed from a seed company, but they also saved some seed from their crops to plant the next spring. Before tractors, they used horses and mules, which they could breed themselves. They got fertilizer from their animals' waste or learned to rotate crops to put nitrogen and other nutrients back in the soil. A farm was a largely independent operation.

Machinery, store-bought seeds and fertilizer, pesticides, and the like have made the modern farm an incredibly productive place. But they've also made the farmer incredibly dependent, and often saddled with debt. The flood of pesticides, herbicides, and artificial fertilizer harms the farmer's health, erodes the soil, ruins its fertility, pollutes the groundwater, and damages the safety of the food we eat. This is the great trade-off of modern agriculture—enormous productivity, but at what cost?

The NewLeaf potato and other GMO crops represent another big step in the same direction. By agreeing to plant them, farmers have to give up yet more of their independence, and put themselves even more at the mercy of agribusiness. Of course, Monsanto has another view of it. They say that genetically engineered plants like the NewLeaf will reduce chemicals in the environment. Instead of buying expensive toxic chemicals, farmers can buy expensive bioengineered plants that make their own toxins.

Is that model better? Is it healthier for the farmer, the consumer, or the environment? Are genetically engineered plants the solution to the problems with our food supply, or are they more of the same? A "solution" that creates new problems?

The First Spuds

The patented potatoes I was planting were descended from wild ancestors growing on the slopes of the Andes Mountains in South America. It was there that *Solanum tuberosum* was first domesticated more than seven thousand years ago by ancestors of the Incas. Among the different varieties I grow are a couple of ancient heirlooms, similar to ones grown thousands of years ago in the Andes, including a blue potato from Peru. That starchy spud is about the size of a golf ball. When you slice it through the middle the flesh looks as though it has been tie-dyed a beautiful shade of blue.

In addition to the blue potato, the Incas grew reds, pinks,

yellows, and oranges. Their potatoes were all manner of shapes, skinny and fat, with smooth skins or rough. They had potatoes that could go without water in a drought and others that needed lots of rain. Some were naturally sweet and others bitter; these were good for animal feed. They had some three thousand different spuds in all. That is why the Andes were and still are the center of potato diversity, the place botanists go to find the original potato ancestors.

Before the Spanish conquest, the Incas had the most advanced system of agriculture in the world. They had figured out how to grow crops on the slopes of high mountains, where the climate can change every few feet in elevation. Even a small difference in altitude can mean a big difference in sun, water, wind, and temperature. A potato that thrives on one side of a ridge at one altitude will die in another plot only a few steps away. That is why they needed so many different types of potato, each one suited to a different plot of land and a different purpose.

Modern industrial farms are examples of monoculture. (*Mono* comes from the Greek word for one.) They consist of vast fields of just one type of potato or corn or soybean over hundreds of acres. The Incas did exactly the opposite, as do some of their descendants in the Andes today. Instead of attempting to change the environment to grow one type of potato, they changed the potato to grow in many different types of environments. This is called polyculture—the opposite of monoculture.

To modern eyes the result may seem patchy and disorganized. It's nothing like the vast, orderly fields of corn or soybean that can be mowed down and harvested with giant machines. There are a few plants over here and a few different ones over there. The traditional Andean potato farm represents a very different approach to agriculture. It blends with nature instead of trying to overcome it. That makes it very tough and long-lasting in the face of storms, drought, or other natural events.

The diversity of a traditional Andean potato farm goes beyond its borders. Along the edges of the potato plots grow lots of wild potato "weeds." The potatoes the farmer has planted sometimes crossbreed with their wild cousins. Sometimes this produces a new variety of potato that does even better in that plot. If it does, the farmer simply starts planting that new hybrid.

In this way the potato in the Andes continually evolves, drawing on the rich treasure house of potato genetic diversity without the aid of scientists working in a lab. And unlike my NewLeaf potatoes, these new varieties don't come with warning labels. The farmers are free to use them and share them as they wish.

Potato Gold

Francisco Pizarro and the Spanish conquerors who enslaved the Incas weren't looking for the potato. They didn't even know it existed. They were only interested in gold, and they managed to take plenty of it out of the Americas and back to Europe. But in the end, the potato proved to be much more valuable than any other treasure they took. Transplanted first to Europe and then to the rest of the world, it became, with human help, one of the major food crops on the planet.

The first potato arrived in Europe sometime around 1600, probably as an afterthought in the hold of a Spanish ship. At first, it had trouble being accepted. The problem was not with the European soil or climate, which would prove very much to the potato's liking (in the north anyway). The problem was the European mind. The potato ran into some strong prejudices.

Europeans didn't eat many root vegetables. Their main crops were grains like wheat and barley. The potato is a member of the nightshade family (along with the tomato), and nightshade leaves are toxic. They were said to cause leprosy and immorality. It came from America, where it was eaten by indigenous people who were seen as inferior. For these and other reasons, the potato got a bad reputation.

The exception was in Ireland. The Irish embraced the potato very soon after its introduction. One story says that happened thanks to a shipwreck of a Spanish galleon off the Irish coast in 1588. Whether that story is true or not, Ireland proved to be an ideal home for the plant.

Grains grow poorly on the island (wheat hardly at all), and in the 1600s the English seized what little good farmland there was for English nobility. This left the Irish peasants with land that was so rain-soaked and poor that virtually nothing would grow on it. Then along came the potato. It not only thrived in Ireland's climate, but it could also produce enormous amounts of food from the very land the English had given up.

The Irish discovered that a few acres of otherwise unfarmable land could produce enough potatoes to feed a large family and its livestock. The Irish also found they could grow potatoes with a bare minimum of labor or tools. They learned to plant something called a "lazybed." The spuds were simply laid out in a rectangle on the ground. Then, with a spade, the farmer would dig a trench on either side of his potato bed, covering the tubers with whatever soil, sod, or peat came out of the trench.

This produced plenty of potatoes, but made for farms with no plowed earth, no neat rows of grain. To the English nobility this was poor farming. The potato vines were sloppy and disorganized. Wheat and grains pointed up to the sun, potatoes grew down into the earth. The English at that time had terrible prejudice against the Irish, who they said were uncivilized. The potato was seen as an uncivilized food, not truly fit for human beings.

The Irish were too hungry to worry about English prejudice. In fact, the potato gave them more control over their lives. With the spuds, they could feed themselves and not worry about the price of bread or wages set by the English. For the Irish had discovered that a diet of potatoes supplemented with cow's milk was all the human body needed. In addition to energy in the form of carbohydrates, potatoes supplied considerable amounts of protein and vitamins B and C. Before the potato, poor people across Europe suffered from scurvy, a disease that comes from lack of Vitamin C. The potato would eventually put an end to scurvy in Europe.

All that was missing from the potato was vitamin A, and that could be supplied by a bit of milk. So, it turns out that mashed potatoes with milk or butter are not only the ultimate comfort food, but all a body really needs. And as easy as they were to grow, potatoes were even easier to prepare. Just dig, heat—by either boiling them in a pot or simply dropping them into a fire—and eat.

The Potato Conquers Europe

Eventually the potato would win over all of northern Europe. But it had to struggle for acceptance. In Germany, King Frederick the Great had to *force* peasants to plant potatoes. In Russia, Empress Catherine the Great had to do likewise. In France, King Louis XVI (living in Versailles) took a different approach. He reasoned that if he could make the potato seem like a food of the nobility, then everyone would want it.

His queen, Marie Antoinette, took to wearing potato flowers in her hair, and Louis ordered a field of potatoes planted on the palace grounds. He posted his royal guard to protect the crop during the day. But he sent the guards home at midnight, leaving the field open. The local peasants, seeing the crop guarded by the king's soldiers, became convinced it was valuable. They snuck onto the unguarded field at night and stole the tubers, then planted them in their own gardens.

In time, all three nations would grow powerful on potatoes. The potato put an end to malnutrition and famine in northern Europe. Potatoes allowed the land to support a much larger population than it could have planted in grain. Since fewer hands were needed to farm it, the potato also freed peasants to leave the countryside and join northern Europe's growing industrial cities. Europe's center of political power had always been in the hot, sunny south, where wheat grew reliably. With the potato, the balance of European power tilted north.

The last holdout of anti-potato prejudice was England. A large portion of the elite in London regarded the potato as nothing less than a threat to civilization. Then in 1794, the wheat harvest in the British Isles failed. The price of bread rose beyond the reach of England's poor. Food riots broke out, and with them a great debate over the potato. The country's leading journalists, farm experts, and political economists all took sides.

Some argued that introducing a new basic crop would feed the poor when bread was expensive. As a side benefit (to the rich) it would keep wages from rising since workers would not need more money to buy bread.

Thanks largely to the food provided by spuds, Ireland's population had grown from three million to eight million in less than a century. Yet some economists saw this as a bad thing. It might be hard for us to believe today, but it was accepted in some circles that starvation was needed to keep the population of the poor in check.

These arguments were mixed with anti-Irish prejudice in England. The Irish were described in newspaper articles as little better than animals, living in filthy windowless huts, with the family pig joining in at dinner. The potato, it was said, had dragged the Irish down into the dirt where it grew.

Today we can see that much of the anti-potato argument was prejudice or pure nonsense. But one point turned out to be true. Some economists thought the potato was a bad crop because it was very difficult to store compared to wheat or corn. People who relied solely on the potato had to count on a new crop every year. For centuries the Irish did just that without problem. Then in the summer of 1845, a fungus arrived in Europe, probably on a ship from America. Its scientific name was *Phytophthora infestans,* but it soon came to be known as the potato blight.

Potato Famine

Within weeks the spores of this savage fungus, borne on the wind, overspread the continent, dooming potatoes and potato eaters alike. The fungus could cover a field literally overnight. First there would be a black spotting of the leaves. Then an ugly stain would appear, spreading down the plant's stem. Quickly, the fungus reached the tubers in the ground, which would rot and turn into evil-smelling slime. It took but a few days for the fungus to scorch a green field black; even potatoes in storage were destroyed. All of this was accompanied by a terrible stench of rotting food.

The potato blight visited all of Europe, but only in Ireland did it produce widespread hunger and starvation. Elsewhere, people could turn to other foods when a crop failed. Ireland's poor lived only on potatoes and had no money to buy grain or bread.

The potato famine was the worst catastrophe to befall Europe since the Plague of 1348, also known as the Black Death. A million Irish died of starvation in three years. That was more than one-tenth of the population. Thousands of others went blind or insane for lack of vitamins potatoes had supplied.

Descriptions of the famine in Ireland read like visions of Hell. The streets were piled with corpses no one had the strength to bury. Whole villages stood deserted. Disease followed on famine: Typhus, cholera, and other illnesses raced unchecked through the weakened population.

As is often the case in times of starvation, the problem was not quite so simple as a shortage of food. At the height of the famine, Ireland's docks were heaped with sacks of corn destined for export to England. But the potato eaters had no money to pay for corn. It was sold elsewhere, and Ireland's poor were left to die.

The laws made anyone who owned more than a quarter acre of land ineligible for aid from the government. That forced millions of Irish to give up their farms in order to eat. Those who had energy and money for a ticket left for America. Within a decade, Ireland's population was cut in half, while the Irish joined the tide of immigration to the United States.

There was enough food to eat, but the poor had no money to buy it. The economy and the government were controlled by the English nobility who had no sympathy for the Irish. Relief efforts were scattered and half-hearted. Yet at the bottom of it all was a simple fact about the potato and Ireland: The country was a giant example of the perils of monoculture. Not only did the agriculture and diet of the Irish depend utterly on the potato, and no other crop, but they depended on just one kind of potato: the Lumper.

Just like in my own garden, potatoes on a farm aren't grown from seed, but from a piece of an older potato. That meant that every Lumper potato in Ireland was a clone, genetically identical to every other Lumper. All of them were descended from a single plant that just happened to have no resistance to the fungus that caused the blight.

The Incas too built a civilization atop the potato, but theirs was the opposite of a monoculture. No one fungus could ever have spread through every little plot and different potato variety. In fact, in the aftermath of the famine, breeders went to the Andes to look for potatoes that could resist the blight. And they found one, a potato called the Garnet Chile.

The Fishamato?

The tragedy of the potato famine and the dangers of monoculture were never far from my thoughts as I waited for my NewLeaf potatoes to poke their shoots out of the ground. In May, after several days of drenching rain, the sun appeared, and so did my NewLeafs. A dozen deep green shoots pushed up out of the soil and started to grow—faster and more forcefully than any of my other potatoes. But apart from their speed, my NewLeafs looked perfectly normal. They certainly didn't beep or glow, as a few visitors to my garden jokingly suggested.

With genetic engineering, the natural limits of change have exploded. For the first time, scientists can bring qualities from anywhere in nature into the DNA of a plant. My friends were joking, but researchers at the Massachusetts Institute of Technology, or MIT, have indeed created glowing tobacco plants. They did this by taking genes from a firefly and inserting them into the DNA of the tobacco plant.

Scientists have inserted a gene from a fish (the flounder) into tomato plants. The flounder, like many fish, produces a protein that keeps its cells from freezing in cold water. By putting the flounder's genes into tomato DNA, the scientists hoped to produce a freeze-proof tomato. That particular bioengineered plant has never been sold to the public, but it's an example of what modern science can do.

Likewise, a tiny but important bit of the NewLeaf potato isn't potato—it's bacteria. The potato didn't evolve the ability to produce Bt insecticide; we gave it that ability. Or rather, we took that ability from bacteria and gave it to the plant.

This may seem strange, even creepy, but the boundaries between different organisms have never been as sharp as we might think. It's likely that some of the DNA in our cells originally came from bacteria. Still, that DNA has evolved with us for millions of years. The NewLeaf Bt-producing potato is brand-new. We don't really know how it will interact with other plants.

How will it affect the environment? What will it do to people (maybe me) who choose to eat it?

The Gene Gun

In search of some of those answers, I decided to visit the birthplace of the NewLeaf, Monsanto headquarters in St. Louis. The company was founded in 1901 and at one point, thanks to its many herbicides, pesticides, and other products, was one of the biggest chemical manufacturers in the United States. It was also one of the first companies to use bioengineering to create genetically modified organisms and bring them to market.

The headquarters is a low-slung brick building on a bank of the Missouri River. It would look like any other corporate complex if not for its stunning roofline. From a distance the roof shimmers like a castle made of glass. Those are the twenty-six greenhouses that crown the building in a dramatic sequence of triangular peaks.

The first generation of GMO plants were grown under this roof, starting in 1984. At the time, it was one of a small handful of places where the world's crop plants were being redesigned. The greenhouses were built because in the early days of biotechnology, no one was sure if it was safe to grow the plants outdoors, in nature.

Dave Starck, one of Monsanto's senior potato people, escorted me through the rooms where potatoes are genetically engineered.

He explained that there are two ways of splicing genes into a plant. One way is by shooting it with a gene gun, which really is a gun. Bullets dipped in a DNA solution are fired at a stem or leaf of the target plant. If all goes well, some of the DNA will pierce the wall of some of the cells' nuclei and elbow its way inside. If the new DNA happens to land in the right place the plant grown from that cell will carry the new gene. It's brutal, but it works.

The second, less violent way Monsanto used to get new DNA into a plant is to infect it with agrobacterium. That is a type of bacteria that naturally evolved the ability to place some of its DNA into a plant. Bacteria are masters of gene transfer, and the agrobacterium is especially good at it.

To create a Bt-producing potato, the Monsanto scientists first place the Bt gene in the agrobacterium. Then the agrobacterium infects a piece of potato plant stem and inserts the gene for making Bt into the plant's DNA.

In addition to the Bt gene, Monsanto inserts a second, "marker" gene into the plant. The marker allows Monsanto to easily test any potato to see if it's a NewLeaf. It's like a genetic QR code. That marker would allow Monsanto to find out if I broke the law and planted a second generation of the potatoes in my garden. I don't expect to see potato police show up in my backyard, but I suppose they could.

After several hours the potato stems begin to put down roots. A few days later, these plantlets are moved upstairs to the potato greenhouse on the roof. I went upstairs and met Glenda Debrecht, a cheerful staff scientist. She invited me to put on latex gloves and help her transplant the pinkie-sized seedlings to small pots filled with soil. After the high tech of the laboratory, it was a relief to be in a greenhouse handling actual plants.

The whole operation is performed thousands of times, Glenda explained. That's because there is so much uncertainty about the outcome. The way genes work is only just beginning to be understood. For example, no gene works by itself. It works in company with other genes that regulate when the gene is active or not. Scientists say these companions regulate the gene's *expression*. That means it's not enough for scientists to transfer one gene. They have to make sure the whole group of genes is present and working together correctly.

Freaky Plants

Natural cell reproduction is an incredibly complex and elegant process. Using agrobacteria or a gene gun is anything but precise. It often results in what is called "genetic instability." That means genes that end up in the wrong place in the genome or are expressed in ways the scientists didn't expect.

In a mild case, that can mean there is too much or not enough Bt being produced in the plant. In a more severe case, the plant grows in strange and unhealthy ways. The process can fail as much as 90 percent of the time. As a result, Glenda told me she sees a great many freaky potato plants.

"We grow out thousands of different plants," Glenda explained, "and then look for the best." The result often can't be explained. My NewLeafs, for example, aren't simply toxic to beetles; they grow faster and stronger. That's good, I suppose, but the scientists at Monsanto couldn't explain how that happened. It was an accident.

That made me wonder what other accidents the scientists might produce. The technology was at the same time both very sophisticated and still a shot in the dark. Their method seemed to be to throw a bunch of DNA against the wall and see what sticks. Do this enough times and you're bound to get what you're looking for.

"There's still a lot we don't understand about gene expression," Starck admitted. A great many factors influence whether, and to what extent, a gene will do what it's supposed to do. In one early experiment, scientists succeeded in splicing a gene for redness into petunias. In the field everything went according to plan, until the temperature hit 90 degrees and an entire planting of red petunias suddenly turned white—no one could say why.

Bt and Butterflies

When I got home from St. Louis, my potato crop was thriving. It was time to build little mounds around the plants, or "hill them up." Using a hoe, I piled rich soil around the stems to protect the developing tubers from the light. I also threw on a few shovelfuls of old cow manure: Potatoes seem to love the stuff. Once, as a teenager, I helped a neighbor dig some spuds out of the pile of pure horse manure he'd planted them in. Those were the best, sweetest potatoes I ever tasted. I sometimes think it must have been this dazzling example of magic that sold me on gardening. Something wonderful to eat grown from something very much not wonderful.

My NewLeafs were big as shrubs now and crowned with slender flower stalks. Potato flowers are actually quite pretty, five-petaled lavender stars with yellow centers that give off a faint roselike perfume. One sultry afternoon I watched the bumblebees making their rounds of my potato blossoms, chalking themselves with yellow pollen grains before lumbering off to other blossoms. The pollen, like every other part of the plant, contains Bt toxin.

Potatoes aren't the only crop that has been engineered to produce Bt. Tens of millions of acres have been planted with Bt-producing corn. Pollen from Bt corn is deadly to the caterpillars of Monarch butterflies. Monarchs don't eat corn pollen, they only eat the leaves of milkweed. But here's the catch: Milkweed is very commonly found in American cornfields. There's nothing to stop corn pollen from blowing over onto the leaves of milkweed, where it can poison Monarch caterpillars.

After decades of use, there is still debate about whether Bt from corn really harms butterflies. The US Department of Agriculture says their studies show that not enough of the pollen reaches the Monarchs to be a problem. If true, then that is one less thing to worry about when it comes to bioengineered plants.

The Silent Spring

There is a long, sad history of unexpected harm to the environment from chemicals and technology we were told was safe. A good example is the once widely used pesticide called DDT.

DDT was the first manufactured chemical pesticide. When it was introduced in the 1940s it was seen as a wonderful tool for controlling malaria and other diseases carried by insects. In fact, the Swiss chemist who discovered it could kill insects was awarded the Nobel Prize. DDT was thoroughly tested and thought to be safe and so it was widely used in agriculture and in homes.

What scientists didn't know or didn't consider was that DDT lasts for a long time in the environment. It builds up over time in the bodies of small birds and other animals. One of its effects is to thin out the eggshells of birds, causing them to break when adult birds brood or sit on them. Because hawks, eagles, and other birds of prey eat lots of little birds and animals, they got an especially high dose of the DDT.

In 1962, the environmentalist Rachel Carson wrote a groundbreaking book called *The Silent Spring*. She raised the alarm that bird populations were declining everywhere and said it was because of the use of chemical pesticides. Some researchers had already begun to suspect that the culprit was DDT. They also found possible links between DDT and human health problems. In 1972, the chemical was banned by the US government.

DDT was an example of *unintended consequences*. A chemical or technology is introduced to help with one problem but creates another one, not foreseen by the inventors. There are many examples of this, and they often follow the same pattern as DDT. The new invention is said to be safe until we find out it isn't.

Hoping not to encounter that sort of surprise again, scientists have been busy trying to imagine the unintended consequences that genetically modified crops might cause. One area of concern is "gene flow." That means that genes could jump from the genetically altered plant to another, closely related species.

The bumblebees in my garden are carrying Bt genes, moving from blossom to blossom. Could the genes in that pollen jump to another plant?

Not Ready for Roundup

We already have proof that gene flow can happen, not with Bt-producing potatoes, but with a different type of bioengineered crop, Roundup-Ready Canola (aka rapeseed), also made by Monsanto. These are called Roundup-Ready plants because they are resistant to the weed-killer Roundup. Roundup is the brand name for the chemical glyphosate, a powerful herbicide. It will kill a very broad range of weeds, but unfortunately for farmers and gardeners, it also kills a very broad range of other plants, including crops that haven't been engineered to resist it. Guess who makes Roundup? Monsanto.

Roundup-Ready soybeans and other crops were introduced in 1996. They're genetically engineered to resist Roundup. Farmers can spray Roundup-Ready soybeans with glyphosate and they will survive. You can see the marketing plan—Monsanto (today Bayer) sells farmers Roundup and also sells them the plants that can survive Roundup.

The concern is that if Roundup-Ready genes somehow got into weeds, they too would become resistant to the weed killer. But gene flow is not the only way weeds can acquire resistance to Roundup. Whenever a farmer uses any pesticide over and over again, resistance is bound to emerge. The same thing happens with antibiotics: Whether through mutation or sheer chance, there will always be a small number of individuals in the pest population that happen to possess resistance. The more the farmer sprays the pesticide, the better it is for the resistant pest, whose population explodes. This is exactly what has happened with Roundup. More than fourteen types of superweeds that are resistant to glyphosate have been found in US fields since Roundup-Ready crops were introduced.

These crops were supposed to be better for the environment by allowing farmers to spray less weed killer. But as weeds grow resistant to Roundup, farmers wind up spraying more. This may be an unintended consequence, but it is certainly not an unforeseeable one.

In recent years Roundup-Ready crops have fallen out of favor. Glyphosate (Roundup) has now been linked to cancer in humans. Monsanto and then Bayer were forced to pay several billion dollars in damages to consumers who used Roundup, some of whom developed cancer as a result. Now Bayer is taking Roundup off the market for home use.

Jumping genes and superweeds point to a new kind of environmental problem: "biological pollution." We're already familiar with one form of biological pollution: invasive exotic species such as kudzu, zebra mussels, and Dutch elm disease. These manage to travel from one ecosystem to another, hitching a ride with or sometimes brought by humans. When they arrive in their new homes, they have no natural enemies and can spread unchecked.

Harmful as chemical pollution can be, it eventually disperses and fades, but biological pollution reproduces indefinitely. Think of it as the difference between an oil spill and a disease. Once gene flow creates a new weed or a resistant pest, it can't very well be cleaned up: It's already part of nature.

Weeds aren't the only thing that can evolve. Conventional Bt sprays break down quickly in sunlight and the farmers who use it spray only when confronted with a serious problem. But Bt crops produce the toxin continuously and their Bt doesn't break down as easily. With the environment flooded with Bt, insects that have natural resistance to it have an advantage. They will produce more offspring. Those offspring crowd out their cousins who are not Bt-resistant. Soon you have a new breed of insect that can eat Bt-filled plants without a care.

That is exactly what is happening. Thanks to the flood of Bt in our fields, some insects are becoming resistant to that toxin. Remember, farmers spray crops with Bt. It is the safest insecticide we have. If insects become resistant to it, Bt sprays will no longer work. There is evidence that Bt-resistance is spreading. One study found that several of the major crops' pests around the world had now developed Bt-resistance. Bt is a naturally occurring pesticide. No one owns a patent on it and it's widely used by organic farmers. Careless use of biotechnology by big corporations threatens to rob us of this valuable resource forever.

The War for Potatoes

By July my wait for the first Colorado potato beetle came to an end. I found a gang of larvae, soft brown creatures that are basically beetle caterpillars, munching away happily on the leaves of my ordinary potato plants. I couldn't find a single one of the bugs on my NewLeafs. I kept looking for them, though, and eventually I spied a single mature beetle sitting on a NewLeaf leaf. When I reached to pick it up, the beetle fell drunkenly to the ground. It had been sickened by the plant and would shortly be dead. My NewLeafs were working.

I have to admit to a certain thrill, a feeling of triumph. Any gardener who has battled pests will understand this. Most of us are not in the least bit romantic about the wildlife that assaults our plants, not the bugs or the woodchucks or the deer. To watch a potato plant single-handedly vanquish a potato beetle is, at least from this point of view, a thing of beauty.

My small victory was very much on my mind a few days later when I went to visit potato growers in Idaho. On my flight, from thirty thousand feet up, I could see the perfect green circles formed by the rotating irrigation systems. In some places the

Idaho landscape becomes an endless grid of green coins pressed into the scrubby brown desert.

No one can make a better case for a biotech crop than a potato farmer, which is why Monsanto was eager for me to go to Idaho to meet a few of their customers. From the point of view of an American potato grower, a plant that makes its own pesticide would seem like a godsend. That's because the typical potato field has been doused with so much pesticide that plants wear a dull white coat of chemicals. The soil they grow in is dead, a lifeless gray powder.

Farmers call this a "clean field," since it has been cleansed of all weeds and insects and disease—of all life, that is, with the sole exception of the potato plant. A clean field represents a triumph of human control, but it is a triumph that even many farmers have come to doubt. To such a farmer a new kind of potato that promised to eliminate the need to spray chemicals would be an economic and environmental boon.

I met farmer Danny Forsyth one sweltering morning at the sleepy but well-air-conditioned coffee shop in Jerome, Idaho. Jerome is a one-street, one-coffee-shop town about a hundred miles east of Boise on the interstate. Forsyth is a slight, blue-eyed man in his early sixties with a small, unexpected gray ponytail, and a somewhat nervous manner. He farms three thousand acres of potatoes, corn, and wheat in the area known as the Magic Valley, much of it on land inherited from his father.

He explained the chemistry and economics of modern potato growing for me. When he talks about agricultural chemicals, he sounds like a man desperate to kick a bad habit.

178

"None of us would use them if we had any choice," he said.

I asked Forsyth to walk me through the stages of a growing season. Typically, it begins early in the spring by dosing the soil with a chemical called a fumigant. To control tiny worms and certain diseases in the soil, potato farmers cover their fields with a chemical toxic enough to kill every trace of life in the soil. Next Forsyth puts down an herbicide to "clean" his field of all weeds. Then an insecticide is applied to the soil. Only then are the seedlings planted.

Potatoes and Poison

The insecticide will be absorbed by the young seedlings and for several weeks kill any insect that eats their leaves. When the potato seedlings are six inches tall, a second herbicide is sprayed on the field to control weeds.

Farmers like Forsyth are called dryland farmers. Their land naturally gets very little rain in spring and summer. Some crops, like grapes, do just fine in those conditions. Potatoes, on the other hand, need to be irrigated. On Forsyth's farm that means drawing water from (and returning it to) the nearby Snake River.

The vast green circles I'd seen from the sky are made by giant irrigation machines called pivots. They are formed from sections of pipe joined together and mounted on wheels so they can rotate in a circle. A typical pivot is over 1,300 feet long and covers an area of 135 acres.

The many doses of pesticide, herbicide, and fertilizer are

simply added to the water in the irrigation system. Forsyth's potatoes receive ten weekly doses of chemical fertilizer. Just before the rows close, when the leaves of one row of plants meet those of the next, he begins spraying with a fungicide to control late blight. That is the same blight that caused the Irish potato famine and is once again today the potato grower's most worrisome threat. A single spore can infect a field overnight, Forsyth told me, turning the tubers into a rotting mush.

Beginning in July, around the time I was there, Forsyth hires a crop duster, an airplane to spray for aphids at fourteen-day intervals. The aphids are harmless insects, but they transmit a virus that causes "net necrosis," a brown spotting of the potato's flesh. Despite all his efforts to control it, this happened to Forsyth's crop the year before I visited. Net necrosis is purely cosmetic; it doesn't affect the taste or the health of the potato. But companies like McDonald's know that we don't like to see brown spots on our French fries. So, farmers like Danny Forsyth must spray their fields with toxic chemicals.

The year I was there, that included a pesticide called Monitor.

"Monitor is a deadly chemical," Forsyth told me. It's known to damage the human nervous system. "I won't go into a field for four or five days after it's been sprayed—not even to fix a broken pivot." That is, Forsyth would sooner lose 135 acres of crop to drought than expose himself or an employee to this poison.

Since I visited Forsyth's farm, Monitor has been withdrawn for use in the United States. However, it's merely been replaced by similar chemicals. Many environmentalists believe the entire class of pesticides, called organophosphates, should be banned.

180

Leaving aside the health and environmental costs, the economic cost of all this control is staggering. A potato farmer in Idaho spends roughly $1,950 an acre (mainly on chemicals, electricity, and water) to grow a crop that, in a *good* year, will earn him maybe $2,000. That's how much a french-fry manufacturer will pay for the twenty tons of potatoes a single Idaho acre can yield. It means at most Forsyth can hope to make $50 an acre. It's not hard to see why a farmer like Forsyth would leap at anything that promised fewer sprayings, bioengineered or not.

Before driving out to have a look at his fields, Forsyth and I got onto the subject of organic agriculture. He said some things conventional farmers always say, like, "That's all fine on a small scale, but they don't have to feed the world." But he also said a few things I never expected to hear.

"I like to eat organic food," he told me. "And in fact, I grow a lot of it at the house. The vegetables we buy at the market we just wash and wash and wash. I'm not sure I should be saying this, but I always plant a small area of potatoes without any chemicals. By the end of the season, my field potatoes are fine to eat, but any potatoes I pulled today are probably still full of chemicals. I don't eat them."

Sustainable Farms

After I left the Forsyth farm, I paid a visit to a nearby organic potato grower. Mike Heath is a rugged, quiet man in his mid-fifties. Like most of the organic farmers I've ever met, he looks as though he spends a lot more time outdoors than a conventional farmer, and he probably does. Chemicals are, among other things, labor-saving devices. While we drove around his five hundred acres in a battered old pickup truck, I asked him what he thought about genetic engineering. He voiced many reservations—it was synthetic, there were too many unknowns—but his main objection to planting a biotech potato was simply that as an organic farmer, "it's not what my customers want."

I asked Heath about the NewLeaf potato and the idea of Bt-producing crops. He had no doubt that as a result of introducing so much Bt into the environment, insects would develop resistance. "Face it," he said, "the bugs are always going to be smarter than we are." He felt it was unjust that Monsanto, in search of profits, was willing to ruin Bt as a pesticide.

Heath himself had resorted to spraying Bt on his potatoes only once or twice in the previous ten years. I had assumed that organic farmers sprayed their crops as often as conventional farmers. The difference, I thought, was they just sprayed with different stuff. That turned out to not be the case at all.

Organic farmers like Heath try to make their farms as independent as possible—in other words, self-sustaining. They work to avoid endless rounds of additives, organic or not. Instead, they use methods like complex crop rotation.

Heath has found, for instance, that planting wheat in a field before potatoes "confuses" the potato beetles when they emerge from their larval stage. He also plants strips of flowering plants on the margins of his potato fields—peas or alfalfa, usually. That attracts the beneficial insects that dine on beetle larvae and aphids. If there aren't enough beneficial insects around to do the job, he'll introduce ladybugs.

Heath also grows a dozen different varieties of potatoes, on the theory that biodiversity is the best defense against nature's surprises. A bad year with one variety will likely be offset by a good year with the others. He doesn't, in other words, ever bet the farm on a single crop.

By way of driving home a point, Heath dug up some of his Yukon Golds for me to take home. "I can eat any potato in this field right now." This of course was the opposite of what Danny Forsyth had said: "Most farmers can't eat their spuds out of the field."

For fertilizers, Heath relies on "green manures" (growing cover crops and plowing them under), cow manure from a local dairy, and the occasional spraying of liquefied seaweed. The result is a soil that looks completely different from the other Magic Valley soils I'd fingered that day. Instead of a uniform gray-ish powder, Heath's soil was dark brown and crumbly.

The difference was that this soil was alive. It was full of micro-organisms, mycelium (fungi), worms, insects, and other life. The ecosystem of life in the soil is still not completely understood, yet this doesn't prevent organic farmers and gardeners from nurturing and benefiting from it.

Heath's acres were the very opposite of "clean" fields. There was the occasional weed and loads of insects flitting around. It was all much less neat and ordered. But that was the point. Heath hadn't tried to force absolute order onto the soil. He was trying to work with the ecosystem. He embraced and encouraged diversity, which meant things were going to look a little messier.

Why Not Organic?

On the drive to the airport, I thought about why Mike Heath's farm remains the exception, both in Idaho and elsewhere. Organic farming has really grown since I visited him. In 2019, sales of organic produce reached almost ten billion dollars. There were approximately 16,500 organic farms in the United States. Yet organic farms represent only about 1 percent of the country's total farmland.

The organic model works. Heath spends a fraction as much on pesticide and fertilizer as Danny Forsyth. He produces just as many potatoes—between three and four hundred bags per acre. Heath has to work harder, but he gets more for his organic potatoes.

Yet few of the mainstream farmers I have met consider organic farming a "realistic" alternative. In one way they're right. Our modern way of producing food is built around large, centralized systems. Most of all, it depends on monoculture. Only by planting large fields with a single crop can farming be turned into something that resembles industry. That means very large farms, with very large fields growing just one crop that can be planted and harvested with very large, very expensive machinery. Monoculture creates an illusion of total control. Why an illusion? Because a vast field of identical plants will always be extremely vulnerable to insects, weeds, bad weather, and disease. All the modern chemicals and product developed by corporations are designed to offset the problems of monoculture.

Conventional farmers have been encouraged (or forced) to rely on large corporations to sell them everything, including seed, chemicals, and fuel for their machines. The corporations tell the farmer how and when to use the chemicals. And of course, large corporations (processors) buy the harvest. Large agribusiness corporations promise farmers almost perfect control over their land. The trade-off is that now the corporations control the farmers.

This sort of centralization of agriculture is not likely to be reversed any time soon. For one thing, there's so much money in it. For another, it's so much easier for the farmer to buy prepackaged solutions from big companies. As I said, Mike Heath works a lot harder than Danny Forsyth.

To put the matter simply, a farmer like Mike Heath is working hard to adjust his fields to the logic of nature, while Danny Forsyth is working to adjust his fields to the monoculture system and requirements of industrial farming.

The Perfect Fries

Organic farmers buy remarkably little—some seed, a few tons of manure, maybe a few gallons of ladybugs. They've turned their backs on the system of monoculture industrial farming. For example, I asked organic farmer Mike Heath what he did about net necrosis, the disease that causes spots on potatoes. His answer was simple. "That's only really a problem with Russet Burbanks," he explained. "So I plant other kinds."

He can do that because he's not part of the industrial food chain that supplies big companies like McDonald's, one of the largest buyers of potatoes in the world. That food chain demands Russet Burbanks and nothing else. Why? Because they assume we, the consumers, will buy nothing else. Are they right?

On my way back to Boise I did a drive-through at a McDonald's and ordered a bag of the fries in question. They really were beautiful: slender golden rectangles long enough to overshoot their trim red containers like a bouquet. It's what you expect whenever you go into a McDonald's anywhere in the world. It's why the Russet Burbank is the most successful potato in the world. We've given this plant partner millions of acres of farmland. In return it gives us long, perfect, dependable french fries.

Even while I enjoyed them, I had to ask myself: Is McDonald's giving us the fries we want, or has it created an image of fries and now that's what we expect? Is it our desire for the perfect french fry that drives the global monoculture, or is it just the easiest way for big chains to make and market their fries? Are we willing to settle for something less perfect and uniform? Should we, in fact, demand it?

The Terminator

What I saw on my visit to Idaho were two starkly different approaches to our partnership with plants. In one, as practiced by

Mike Heath and organic farmers, we try to work with our plant partners and with nature. To do this we have to embrace diversity and give up our dream of control. In the other approach, we seek absolute control, sterilizing the soil, treating our plants as raw materials and our farms as factories.

In March 1998, the industrial farm system took another dramatic step in its quest for control. Scientists announced they had bioengineered a soybean plant that had been genetically modified to have sterile seeds. There would be no point in saving seeds to plant the next spring—they were programmed not to grow.

The new kind of plant was quickly given a nickname: "Terminator." With Terminator plants, the agribusiness companies would have complete control. Farmers simply wouldn't be able to save any seed from one year's crop to plant the next spring. They would be forced to come back every year to buy more.

It's true that things have been moving in this direction for a while. Most modern farmers already buy their seed every year. Yet even today, many farmers still retain some seed from their crops, looking for strains that grow well in their fields. This is especially true in other parts of the world, where some 1.4 billion people depend on saved seed to grow their crops the next year.

Technology like Terminator is the ultimate step toward total corporate control. Remember how wild potatoes around the fields in the Andes mix with the planted ones to produce new strains? That kind of hybrid mixing is still possible, as long as the crops we plant can produce living seeds. But if our crops are sterile, then the only place to get new seeds will be from agribusinesses that will sell just one or two varieties of each crop. Say goodbye to biodiversity.

Until recently, it wasn't possible for a company to own the rights to a plant. No one could say they own corn. If you grew your own corn and saved some seed, it was yours to use as you saw fit. That is the way farming worked for thousands of years. But bioengineered crops are patented. You must pay to use the seed every year. Like the NewLeaf potato, you're buying a license to grow it, but the crop doesn't really belong to you.

Agribusiness and many conventional farmers say all of this is necessary. Only modern, industrial, bioengineered farming can grow enough food to feed the world. When I hear that, I think of the Lumper potato and the monoculture that was the root of the potato famine. The people of Ireland thought they knew how to grow enough food to feed themselves, but then disaster struck.

No one can predict what will happen to our industrial monoculture food system. What is clear is that we are rapidly changing the way we grow our food in ways that we couldn't have imagined a short while ago.

There was a loud public outcry against the Terminator bioengineering, so loud that it has never been used. However, agribusiness has developed a replacement that may be even more disturbing. Genetic use restriction technologies (GURT) are a kind of biological on/off switch. The "switch" is a chemical that can be used to turn off fertility in a plant, making its seeds sterile. The switch can also be used to activate other traits. For example, a plant that was engineered to produce Bt would only "work" after it had been sprayed with an activation chemical from the same company. GURT is not currently in use, but you can see how much control it would take away from farmers and give to corporations like Monsanto.

Can Our Partnership Survive?

Soon after my trip to Idaho and my experiment raising my own NewLeaf potatoes, McDonald's and several other large food companies had a change of heart. Responding to growing public unease about GMOs in food, they stopped using them in their products. That appears to have doomed the NewLeaf potato. It is no longer made or planted. However, there are still several other GMO Bt-producing crops, including corn, soybeans, and cotton.

Though NewLeafs may be gone, genetically modified foods seem here to stay. In the United States our basic cash crops, like corn, soybeans, and sugar beets, are almost all GMO plants. Those are widely used in processed foods and animal feed. All of which makes it very likely that you've been eating GMO food.

After many years of battles between consumer activists and GMO producers, in January 2022, the US government established a new rule that requires food companies to label GMO food. Well, sort of. First, instead of GMO, the law allows companies to use the term "bioengineered," which many people don't recognize. Second, it doesn't require an actual label, just a QR code on the package. If you want to find out what's in your food, you have to scan each box or can that you pick up. If you don't have an Internet connection in the supermarket, then you're out of luck.

But in many ways the debate (and worry) about GMOs and bioengineering has shifted. The question is no longer simply whether certain GMO foods are safe for us to eat. The question is much bigger. The industrial food chain is now global. Farmers in Africa, South America, and Asia are being brought into the network of agribusiness, to become dependent on the vast array of chemicals that are needed to grow food in a system of monoculture. GMO crops are just another step in that loss of dependence for farmers everywhere.

We as food consumers should be deeply concerned about this. After all, it's our food, and we literally can't live without it. Is our food supply sustainable? Is it healthy for the environment and for the workers who produce it? Will control of our food continue to be concentrated in the hands of a few powerful corporations? Or will we be able to find another model, one based on cooperation with nature rather than domination of it?

In the past, people made partnerships with plants (and animals). We selected the ones that met our needs and helped them to reproduce and spread. We crossed different varieties to produce new varieties that had traits we needed. It has been a partnership that benefited both us *and* the plants.

But now we have to ask ourselves if that partnership is broken. We are changing the very nature of our plant partners, treating them more as raw materials than as living things. We act as though the balance between humanity and the environment can be ignored. After all, if we can rewrite DNA, why can't we rewrite the rules of nature? Or maybe just ignore them. But history has shown us that nature cannot be controlled in that way, bent to human will. If we disturb the balance of nature too much, both we and our partners will suffer.

There's a growing global movement for justice and fairness in our food system. It's tied to all our other environmental concerns, especially climate change. Let's hope that movement restores some balance and sets our long productive partnership with plants back on a track of cooperation and symbiosis—species in a mutually beneficial relationship.

Turning Over a New Leaf

In August, a few weeks after I got home from Idaho, I dug up my NewLeafs, harvesting a gorgeous-looking pile of spuds. The plants had performed brilliantly, though so had all my other potatoes. The beetle problem never got out of hand, perhaps because the diversity of species in my garden had attracted enough beneficial insects to check the bugs. Who knows? My scapegoat tomatillos may also have helped. A true test would have meant planting a monoculture garden containing nothing but NewLeafs.

By the time I harvested my crop, I realized there was no point in worrying about eating them. The decision had been made for me. Chances were, I'd eaten plenty of NewLeafs already, at McDonald's or in a bag of Frito-Lay chips.

Still, I kept putting off eating the ones I had grown. Maybe because it was August and there were so many more interesting fresh potatoes in my garden—fingerlings with dense, luscious flesh, Yukon Golds (Mike Heath's as well as my own) that looked and tasted as though they'd been buttered in the skin. The idea of cooking with bland commercial Russets seemed almost beside the point.

There was this too: I'd talked to some government agencies, and what they said didn't exactly fill me with confidence. The Food and Drug Administration (FDA) is the government agency that's supposed to guarantee the safety of our food. I'd always assumed the FDA had tested this new potato, maybe fed a bunch of them to rats, but it turned out this was not the case. In fact, the Food and Drug Administration didn't even regard the NewLeaf as a food. *What?*

It seems that since the potato contained Bt, it was, at least in the eyes of the federal government, not a food at all but a pesticide, putting it under the jurisdiction of the Environmental Protection Agency. I phoned the EPA to ask about my potatoes. As the EPA saw it, Bt has always been a safe pesticide, the potato has always been a safe food, so put the two together and you've got something that should be safe both to eat and to kill bugs with.

I was not convinced. I phoned Margaret Mellon at the Union of Concerned Scientists, a nonprofit in Washington, DC, to ask her advice about my spuds. Mellon is a molecular biologist and a leading critic of biotech agriculture. She couldn't offer any hard scientific proof that my NewLeafs were unsafe to eat, but she pointed out that there was also no scientific proof that they *were* safe. She told me, "That research simply hasn't been done."

I pressed: Was there any reason why I shouldn't eat these spuds?

She came back with this: "Let me ask *you* a question: Why would you want to?"

This was a good question. For several weeks my NewLeafs remained in a shopping bag on the porch. There they sat until Labor Day, when I got an invitation to a potluck supper at the town beach. Perfect! I signed up to make a potato salad. The day of the supper, I brought the bag of spuds into the kitchen and set a pot of water on the stove. But before the water even had a chance to boil, I was stricken by this thought: Wouldn't I have to tell people at the picnic what they were eating? And if I did, would anyone eat it?

I turned down the flame under the pot and went out to the garden to harvest a pile of ordinary spuds for my potato salad.

Epilogue: Partners with Nature

Months had passed since I'd planted my potatoes on that warm spring day, listening to the buzzing of the bees. As is always the case by the end of the summer, the garden looked wild and overgrown. The vines, ripe with fruit, were bursting from the neat garden beds and overgrowing the paths. The pole beans had climbed clear to the tops of the sunflowers. The pumpkins had trailed halfway across the lawn, and the squash leaves, big as pizzas, threw dark pools of shade. The lettuces looked happy, as, unfortunately, did the slugs, who were dining on my chard.

The neat, freshly hoed rows had once made it seem that I was in charge here, the gardener-in-chief, but clearly this was no longer the case. My neat order had been overturned as the plants went about their business. They were reaching for the sun, seizing ground from neighbors, and ripening the seeds that would bear their genes into the future.

For a while every season, I try to keep the whole thing under control, pulling the weeds, clipping back the squash, untangling the vines. But by the end of August, I usually give up and let the garden have its way, while I harvest the results. On this late summer morning, I went into the wild mess looking for something, and eventually I found it: a row of Kennebec potatoes. The potatoes were still in the ground, but I could spot them by the wilting leaves sprawled on the dirt.

To me there is no harvest more satisfying than potatoes. I love the moment when the spade turns over the black soil for the first time since spring and the tan lumps tumble out onto the fresh dirt. After gathering up the easy ones, you have to put the spade aside and dig out the rest by hand. Forcing your fingers down into the richly manured soil, you feel around in the dark for those unmistakable shapes. Most potatoes are odd, lopsided things, the opposite of my neatly planned vegetable bed.

Once I'd filled a basket with my spuds, I stood and considered the state of the garden. Whenever I hear or read the word *garden*, I always picture something neat and organized. Every summer I remember the truth. Any healthy garden is its own ecosystem teeming with a wild variety of life. Gardeners merely make suggestions, but it's the plants that decide what happens.

Standing amid the sweet wreck of my garden, lifting a basket heavy with potatoes, I thought about Johnny Appleseed in his coffee sack, about the crazed tulip growers of Amsterdam, the coffee finca owners, and the Monsanto scientists in their lab coats, and wondered what they had in common. All of them, in their own way, had tried to add something to the ongoing partnership between plants and human beings. And all of them had been confronted with the same truth, whether they accepted it or not. *We are not in charge.*

Some of them, like John Chapman or the organic farmer I visited in Idaho, seemed to understand this. Others, like the genetic engineers, believe that farms are just another form of manufacturing. In their view, plants are raw materials to be used or reworked as we see fit.

I keep coming back to the word *partnership*. Understanding that plants are not our servants but our partners is important, because it leads to a bigger understanding: Whether we realize it or not, we are in partnership with the entire natural world.

The environment is not merely a source of raw materials for us to use and discard. Like my garden, like the soil in an organic farm, the earth's environment is a rich, teeming ecosystem, a web of relationships among all sorts of life, relationships that we don't always fully understand. When we ignore these relationships and try to remake the natural world to suit our needs, operating as though we are in control, we wind up destroying that delicate web of life.

Today we see the results of that attitude everywhere—from the giant pile of plastic floating in the middle of the Pacific Ocean, to the sterile monoculture of industrial farming, to the crisis of climate change. We human beings must learn that we are not separate from the natural world, but very much a part of it. We must learn to work with it, as a *partner,* rather than try to use and command it.

I often think about John Chapman floating down the Ohio River, snoozing alongside his mountain of apple seeds. From the tin pot on his head to the bare soles of his feet, he seemed to have understood that we cannot separate ourselves from nature. Though I'm sure he never heard the word *biodiversity,* his piles of wild apple seeds were nothing less than treasure troves of genetic variety and experimentation. I think he was wrong when he said that grafting trees was "wicked," but within that judgment was an important warning not to mess blindly with nature.

We don't have to sleep in a hollow tree or go barefoot all winter to follow Chapman's example. We need to protect diversity in nature, not just in seed banks like the orchards of the Plant Genetic Resources Unit, but in wilderness preserves everywhere on the planet. And like good farmers, we have to accept that our attempts to control nature from on high can never succeed. We must learn that we are, after all, part of nature too. Whatever we do to the natural world will affect us.

We will, of course, continue to plant our gardens and our farms. We will continue to find new ways to get all the things plants offer, whether it's control or sweetness or beauty or energy. That means we will continue to change plants, just as they will continue to change us. This has been going on for thousands of years. There's nothing wrong with using new tools to do this, whether engineering genes or technologies that haven't been invented yet, as long as we use those tools wisely.

Chapman's two-hulled canoe was the perfect symbol of an equal partnership, humans and plants floating along side by side, each balancing the other. That is the balance we must work to maintain: the entire living ecosystem as one interconnected web of life.

We are all in this boat together.

Glossary

angiosperm: a flowering plant. There are approximately 300,000 species of angiosperms, making it the largest group of plants.

biodiversity: the full range of living creatures in an ecosystem.

botany: the study of plants, including their biology, reproduction, categories or types, practical uses, and growth.

cellulose: a type of carbohydrate that makes up the cell walls of plants. Cellulose makes up the woody or tough plant fibers that give plants their structure.

climate change: a change in the long-term weather patterns on Earth caused by large amounts of carbon dioxide and other gases added to the atmosphere by human activity. One effect of climate change is a gradual warming of Earth's atmosphere.

DNA: the chemical compound deoxyribonucleic acid. DNA contains the codes that allow living things to produce proteins and governs how cells function. It is passed from one generation to the next and is the way characteristics are inherited.

domesticated: domesticated plants and animals have adapted to live with or work in partnership with human beings.

ecosystem: a community of organisms that occupy the same area and their physical environment. For example, a lake ecosystem will include all living organisms in and around the lake, along with the water, the soil in the lakebed, and the weather patterns around the lake. An ecosystem might be as small as a puddle of water or as large as the entire Earth.

evolution: the process that produced the wide variety of life on Earth. Living things, though they may look very different, are descended from a common ancestor. Over hundreds of millions of years, species have adapted or evolved through *natural selection*. Individuals who are better suited to an environment are more successful at having offspring and passing on their characteristic to new generations.

gene: a unit of DNA that holds the code for a single protein. Genes are found in long chains of DNA called chromosomes.

herbicide: a chemical that kills plants.

hybrid: the offspring of two different varieties of plants or animals, usually of the same species. For example, the Jonagold apple is a hybrid of Golden Delicious and Jonathan apples.

Industrial Revolution: the period in Europe and the United States when making goods by hand was largely replaced by production by machine, from about 1760 to 1860. During this time, farming also began to be done by machine, and large numbers of people moved from the countryside to the cities.

nectar: a sugar-filled liquid produced by plants to attract insects and animals.

pesticide: a chemical that kills insects or other organisms that are harmful to crops. An *insecticide* is a type of pesticide that targets insects.

pistil: the female organ of a flowering plant. It contains ovules, which become seeds if they are pollinated.

pollen: a fine powder produced by the male organs of plants that contain reproductive cells called gametes. When a grain of pollen lands on a pistil or female organ of a plant, the gamete fertilizes the ovule, and a seed is produced. This is called pollination.

stamen: the male organ of a flowering plant. Stamens produce pollen.

Partial Sources

Listed below, by chapter, are a selection of the principal works that supplied me with facts or influenced my thinking. For a more complete list, see the original edition of *The Botany of Desire*.

INTRODUCTION: THE BEES AND ME

Anderson, Edgar. *Plants, Man and Life*. Berkeley: University of California Press, 1952.

David Attenborough's 1995 public television series *The Private Life of Plants*.

Darwin, Charles. *The Origin of Species,* edited by J. W. Burrow. London: Penguin Books, 1968.

Dawkins, Richard. *The Selfish Gene*. New York: Oxford University Press, 1976.

Diamond, Jared. *Guns, Germs, and Steel: The Fates of Human Societies*. New York: W. W. Norton, 1997.

Wilson, E. O. *The Diversity of Life*. New York: W. W. Norton, 1992.

CHAPTER ONE: THE APPLE

Browning, Frank. *Apples*. New York: North Point Press, 1998.

Crosby, Alfred. *Ecological Imperialism: The Biological Expansion of Europe, 900–1900*. Cambridge, England: Cambridge University Press, 1986.

Martin, Alice A. *All About Apples*. Boston: Houghton Mifflin, 1976.

Price, Robert, *Johnny Appleseed: Man and Myth*. Gloucester, Mass. Peter Smith, 1967.

Thoreau, Henry David. "Wild Apples," in *The Natural History Essays,* introduction and notes by Robert Sattelmeyer. Salt Lake City: Peregrine Smith Books, 1980.

CHAPTER TWO: THE TULIP

Dumas, Alexandre. *The Black Tulip*. New York: A. L. Burt Company, n.d.; first published 1850.

Goody, Jack. *The Culture of Flowers*. Cambridge, England: Cambridge University Press, 1993.

Huxley, Anthony. *Plant and Planet*. London: Penguin Books, 1987.

Pavord, Anna, *The Tulip: The Story of a Flower That Has Made Men Mad*. London: Bloomsbury, 1999.

Pinker, Steven. *How the Mind Works*. New York: W. W. Norton, 1997.

Proctor, Michael, et al. *The Natural History of Pollination*. Portland, Ore. Timber Press, 1996.

CHAPTER THREE: COFFEE AND TEA

Allen, Stewart Lee. *The Devil's Cup: A History of the World According to Coffee*. New York: Soho Press, 1999.

Balzac, Honoré de. *Treatise on Modern Stimulants*. Translated by Kassy Hayden. Cambridge, MA: Wakefield Press, 2018.

Carpenter, Murray. *Caffeinated: How Our Daily Habit Helps, Hurts, and Hooks Us*. New York: Plume, 2015.

Hohenegger, Beatrice. *Liquid Jade: The Story of Tea from East to West*. New York: St. Matin's Press, 2006.

Houtman, Jasper. *The Coffee Visionary: The Life and Legacy of Alfred Peet*. Mountain View, CA: Roundtree Press, 2018.

Pendergrast, Mark. *Uncommon Grounds: The History of Coffee and How It Changed Our World*. New York: Basic Books, 1999.

Sedgewick, Augustine. *Coffeeland: One Man's Dark Empire and the Making of Our Favorite Drug*. New York: Penguin Press, 2020.

Walker, Matthew. *Why We Sleep: Unlocking the Power of Sleep and Dreams*. New York: Scribner, 2017.

CHAPTER FOUR: THE POTATO

Berry, Wendell. *The Gift of Good Land*. San Francisco: North Point Press, 1981.

Fowler, Cary, and Pat Mooney. *Shattering: Food, Politics, and the Loss of Genetic Diversity*. Tucson: University of Arizona Press, 1996.

Holden, John, et al. *Genes, Crops, and the Environment*. Cambridge, England: Cambridge University Press, 1993.

Lewontin, Richard. *Biology as Ideology: The Doctrine of DNA*. New York: Harper Perennial, 1991.

Salaman, Redcliffe. *The History and Social Influence of the Potato*. Cambridge, England: Cambridge University Press, 1985; first published 1949.

Scott, James C. *Seeing Like a State: How Certain Schemes to Improve the Human Condition Have Failed*. New Haven, Conn.: Yale University Press, 1998.

Zuckerman, Larry. *The Potato: How the Humble Spud Rescued the Western World*. Boston: Faber & Faber, 1998.